REMARKABLE ROMANS
&
HISTORICAL MANNEQUIN COSTUMES

COLORING BOOK

Remarkable ROMANS Coloring Book

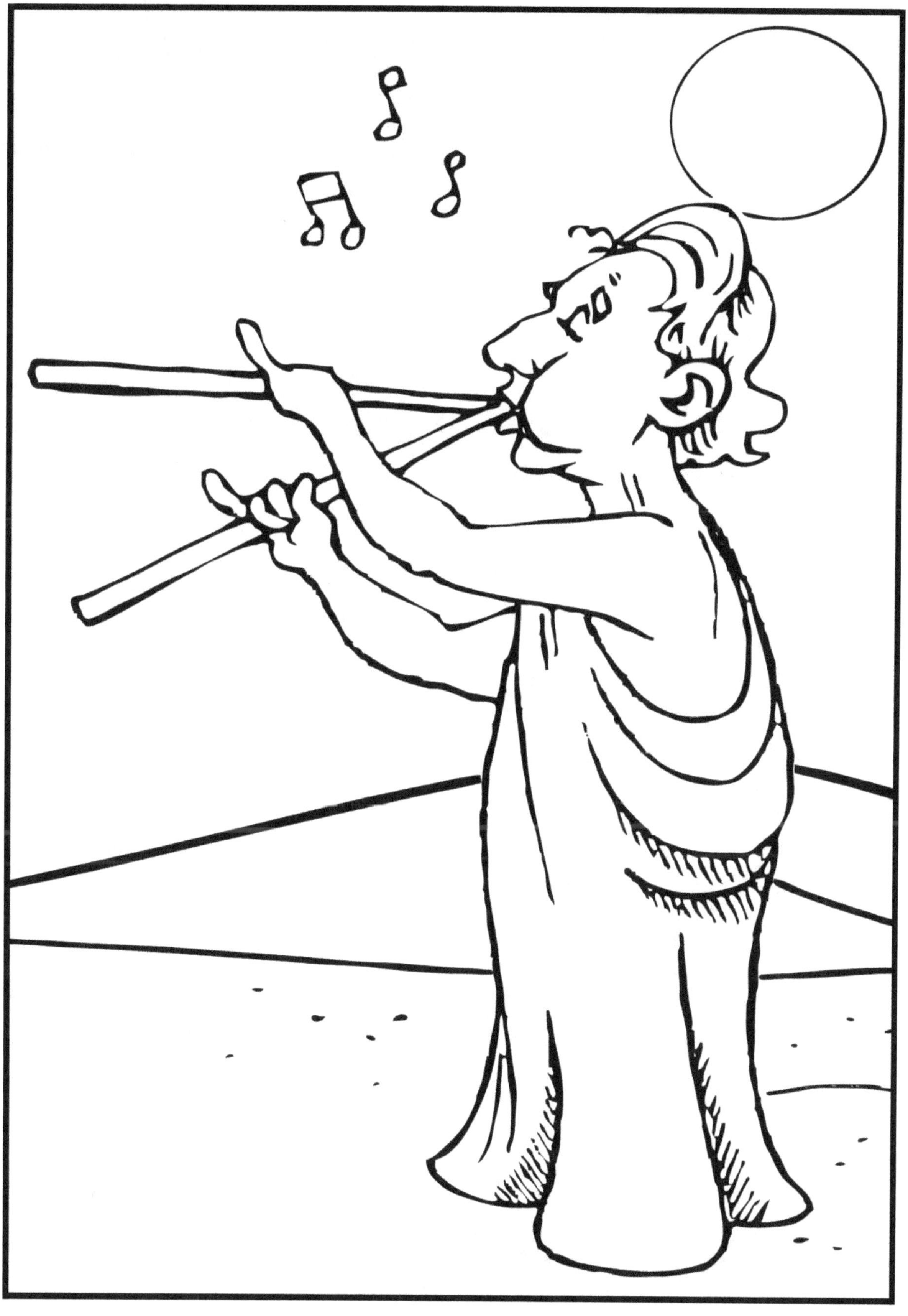

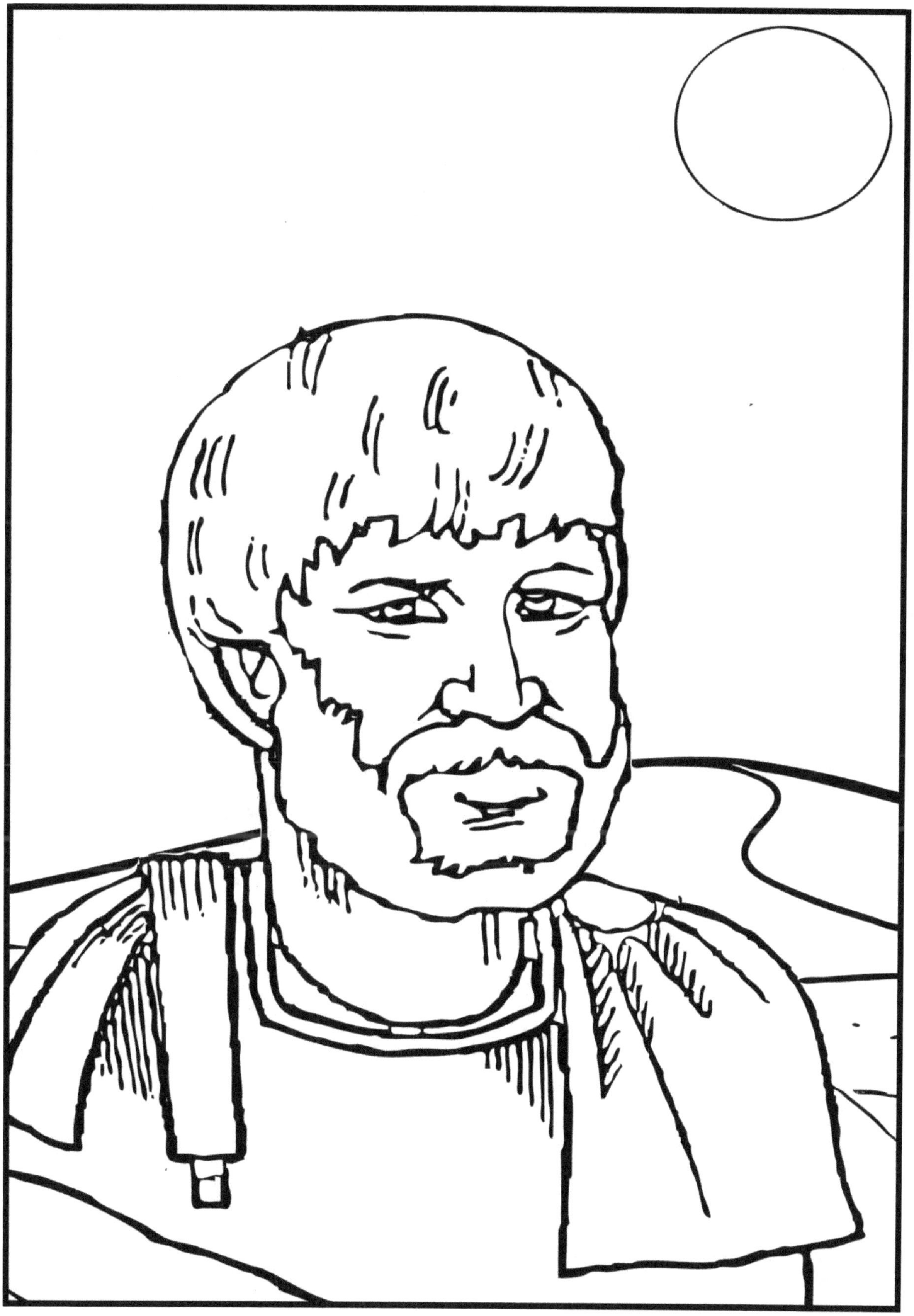

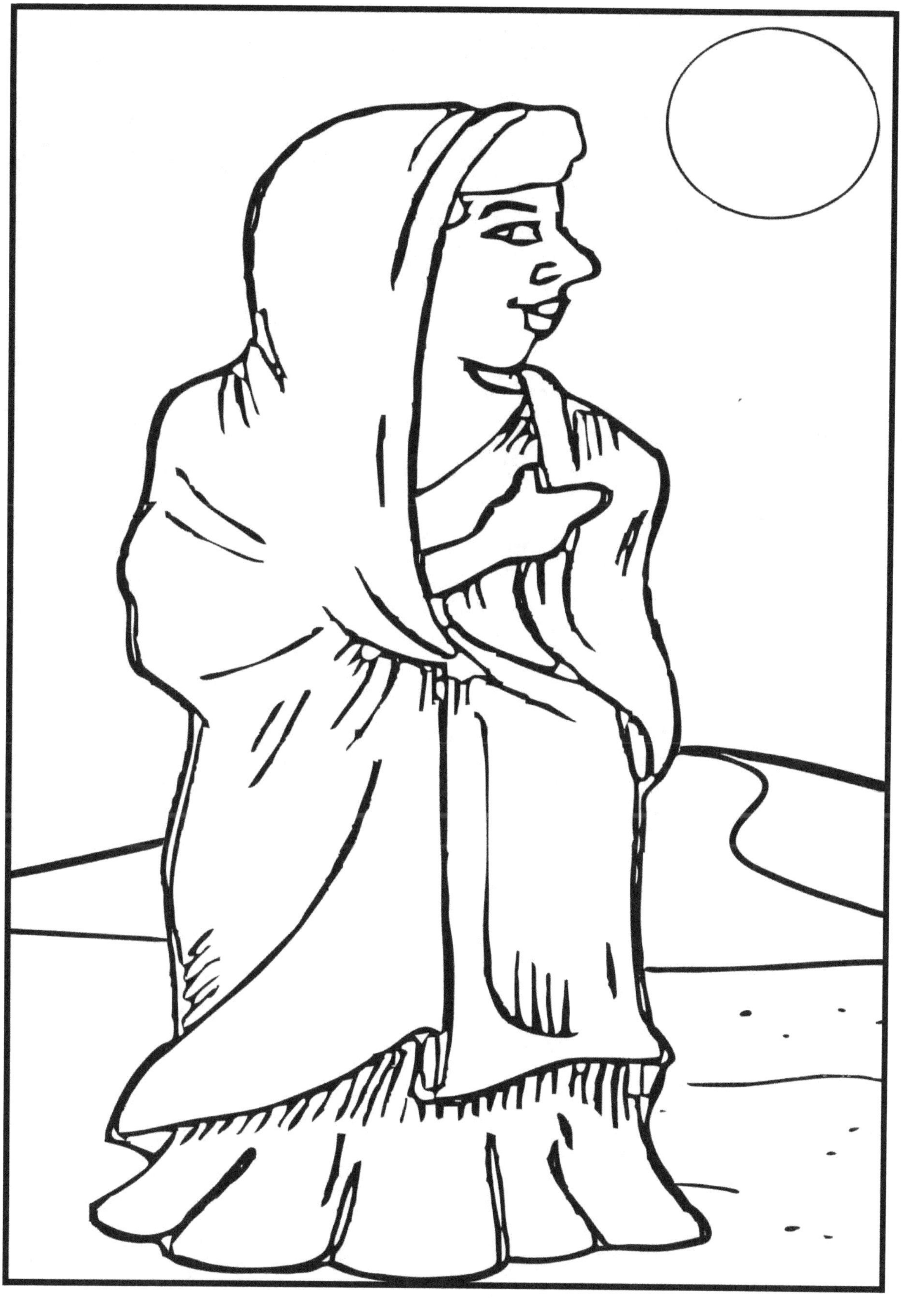

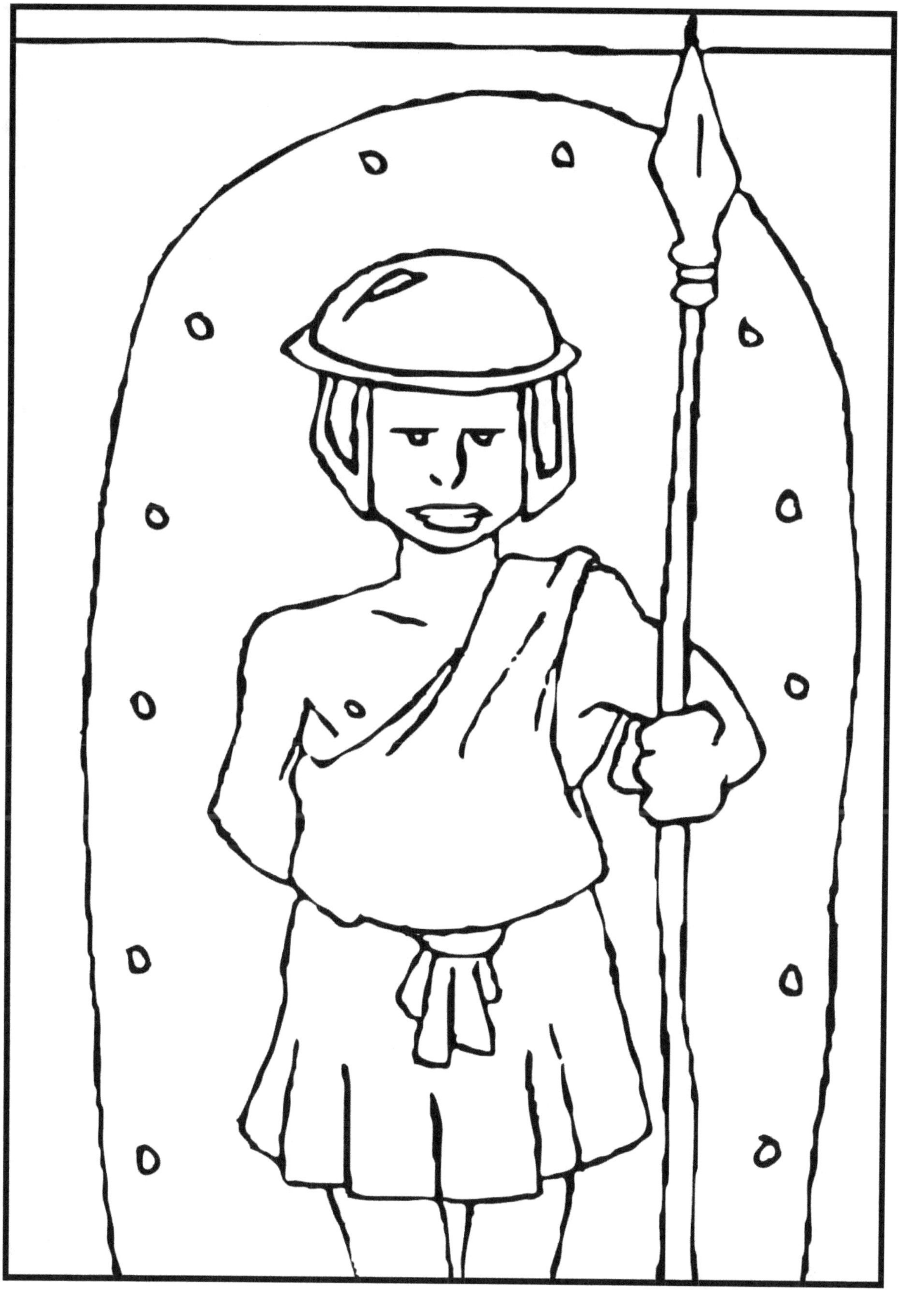

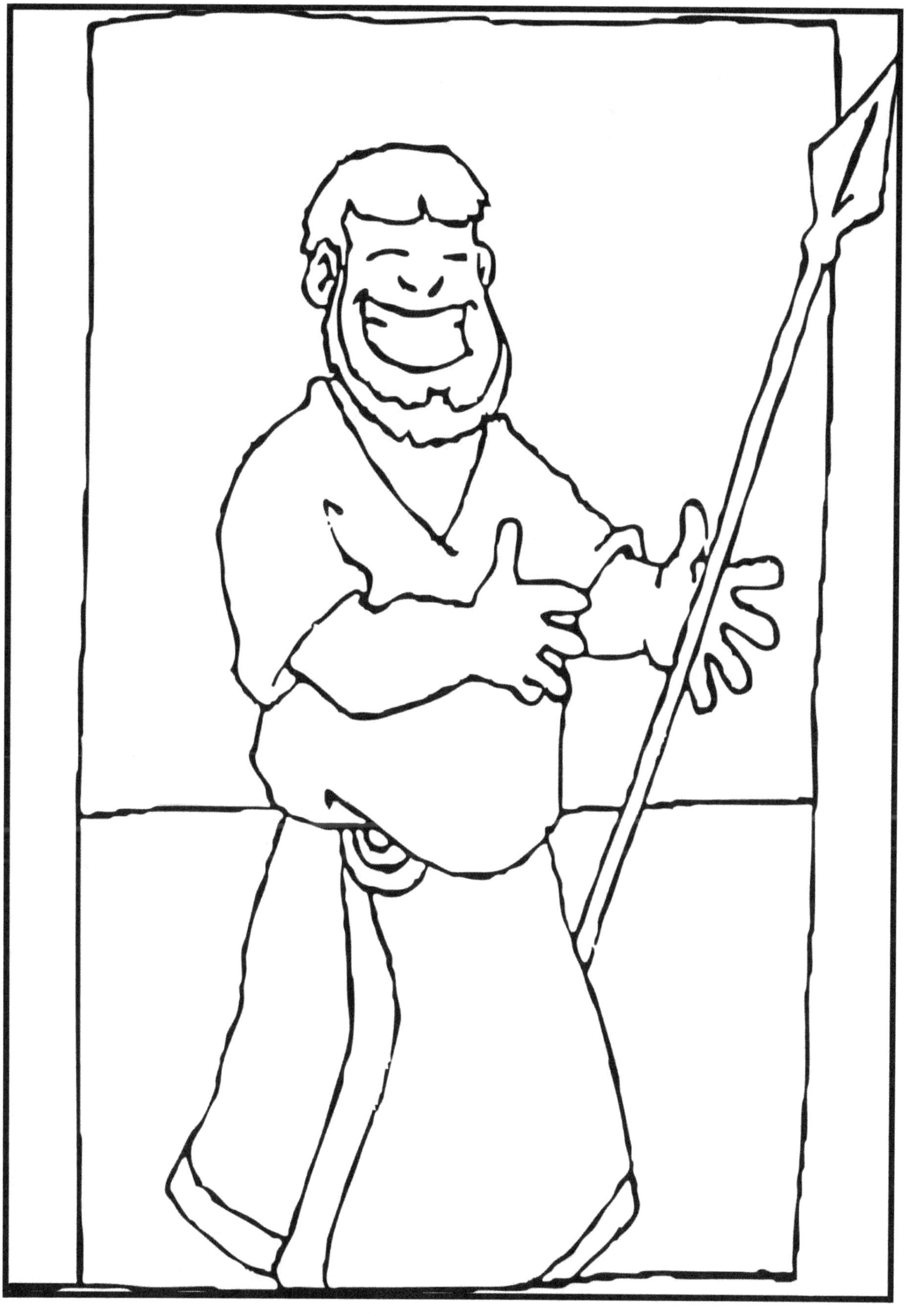

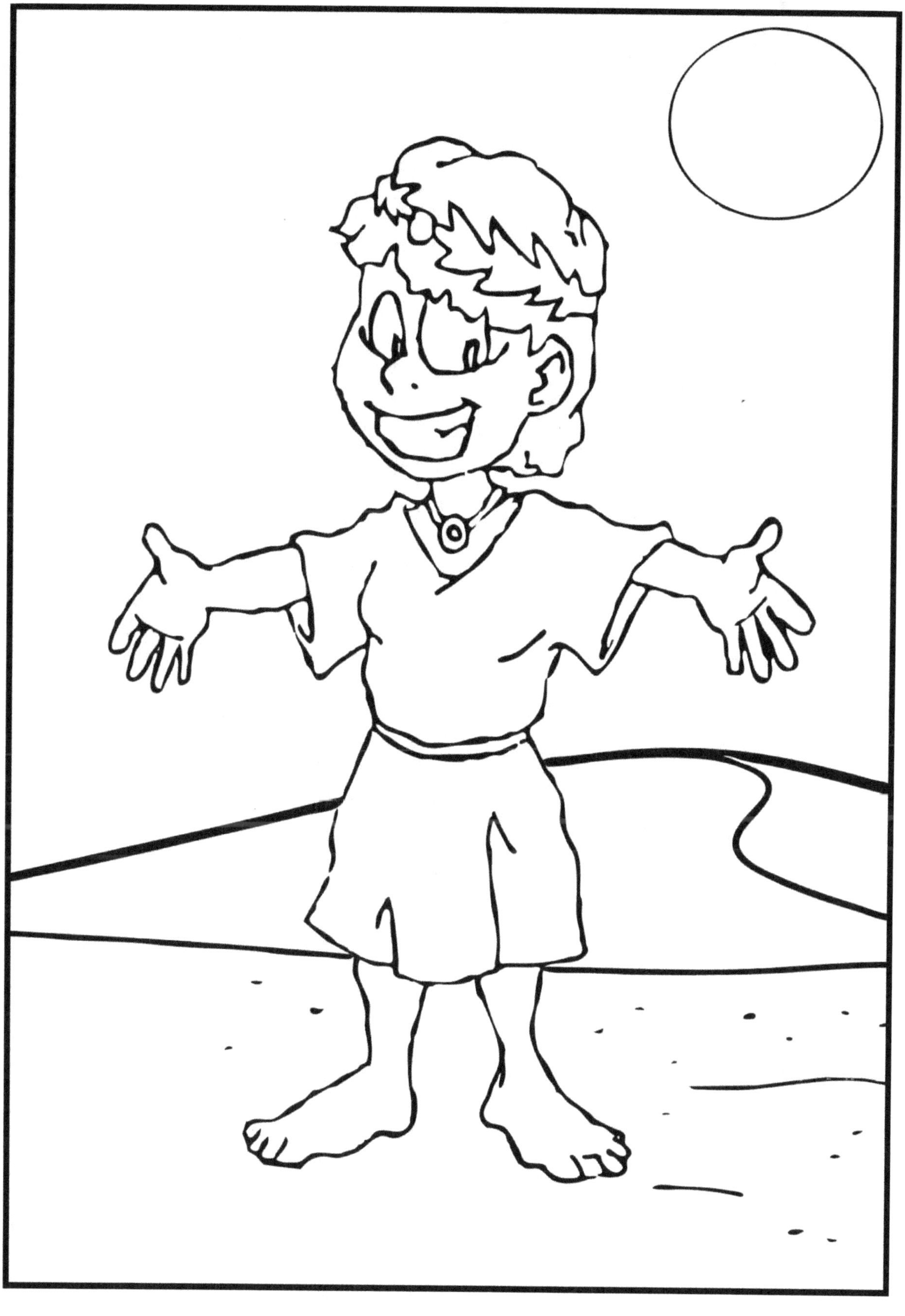

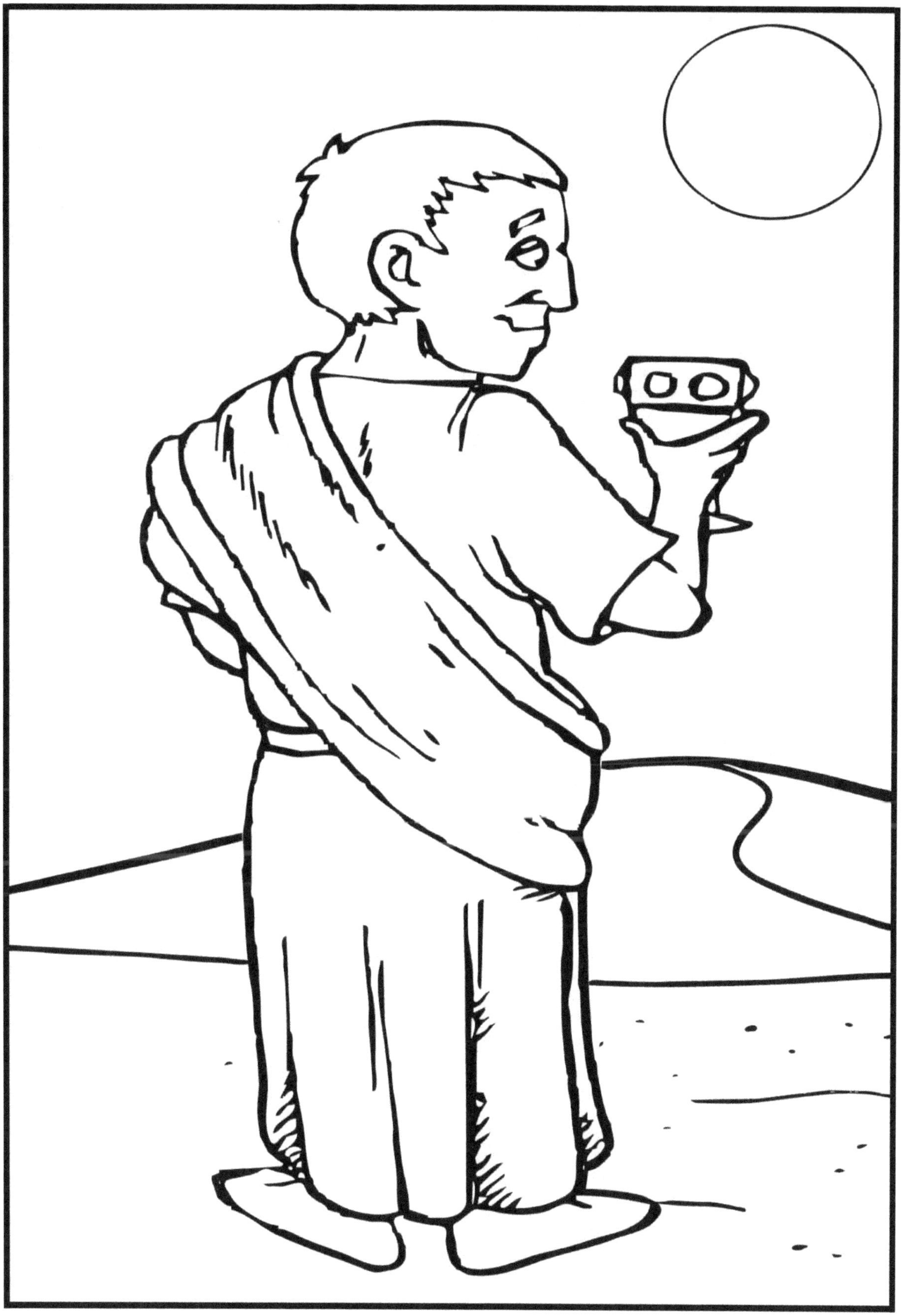

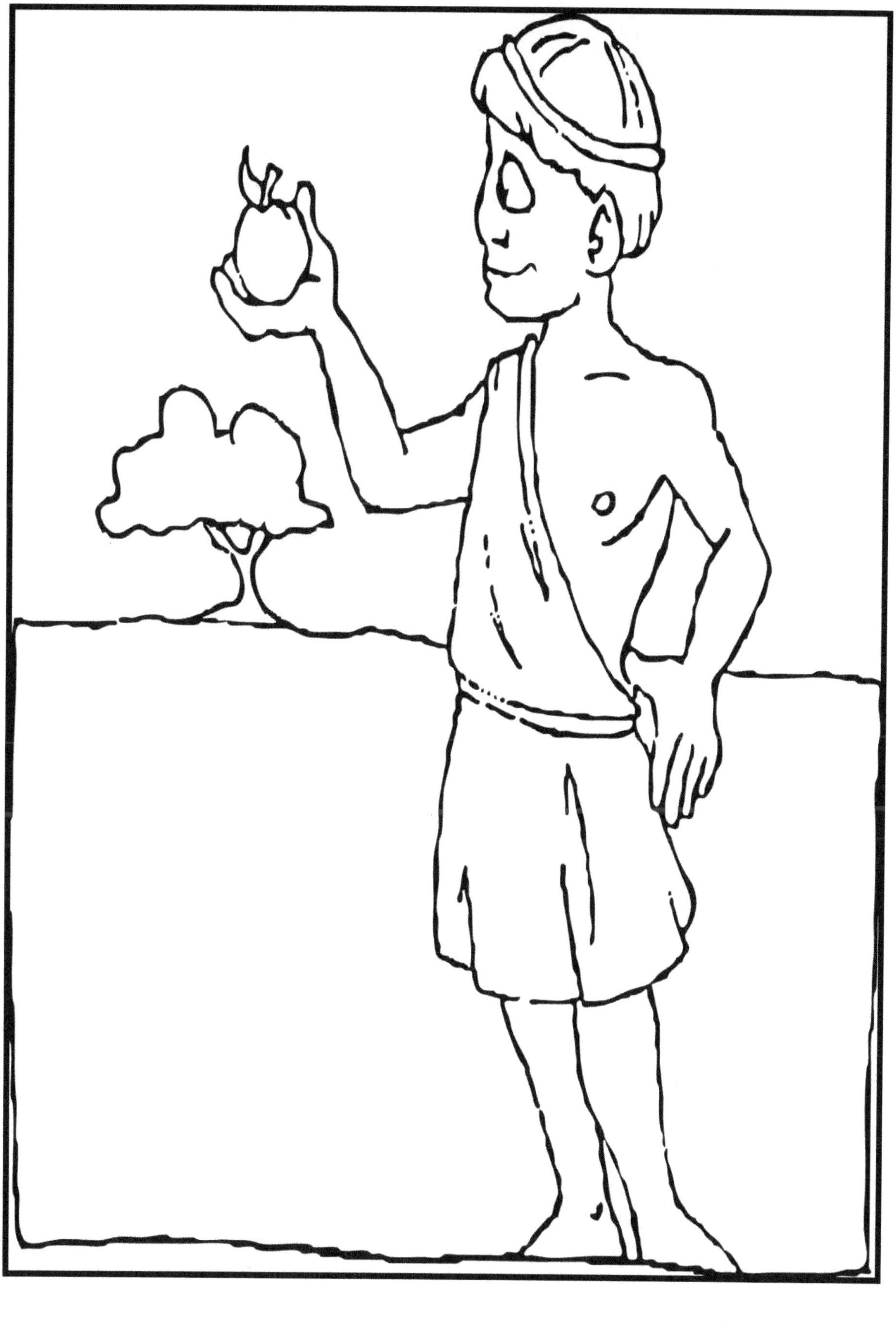

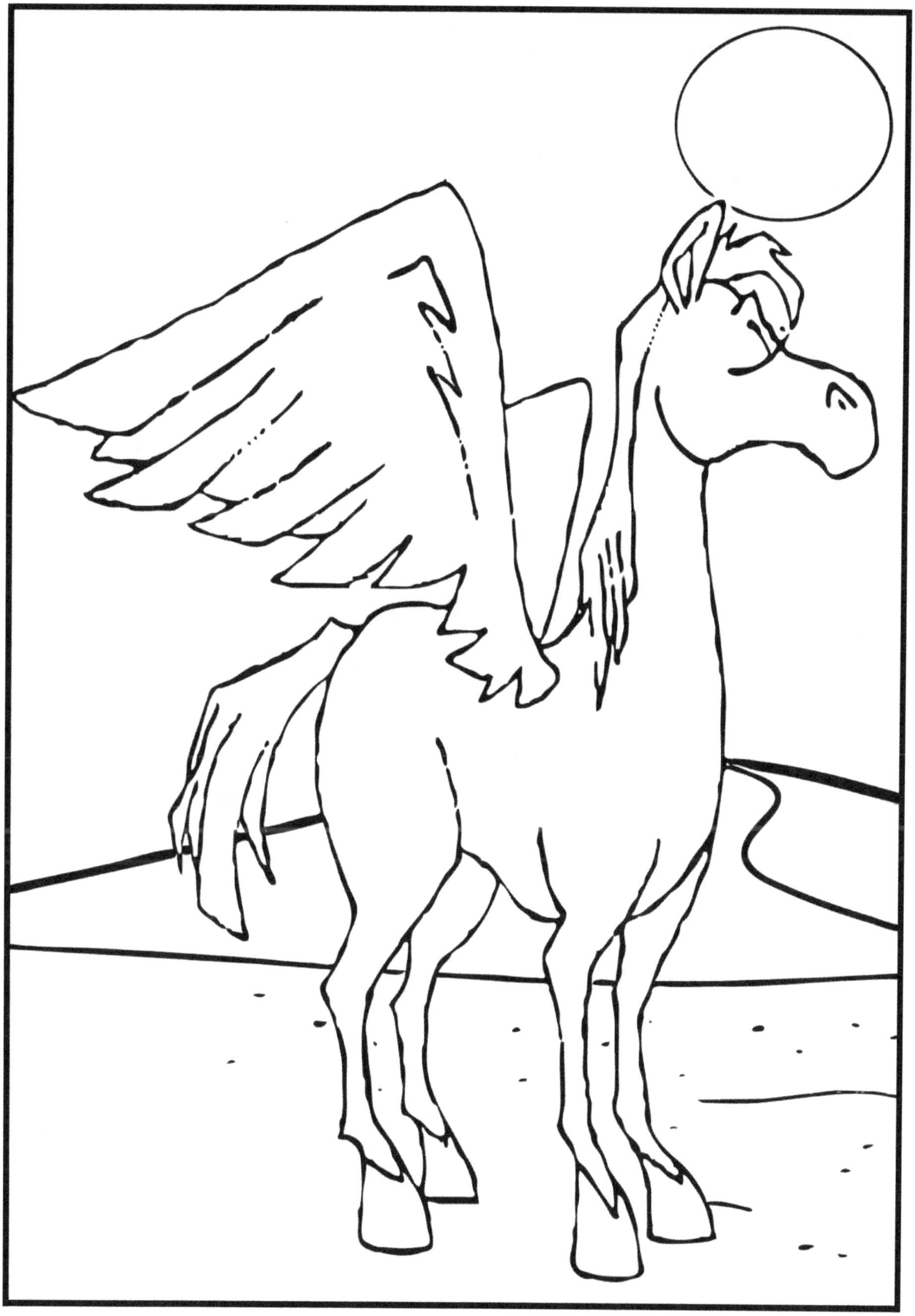

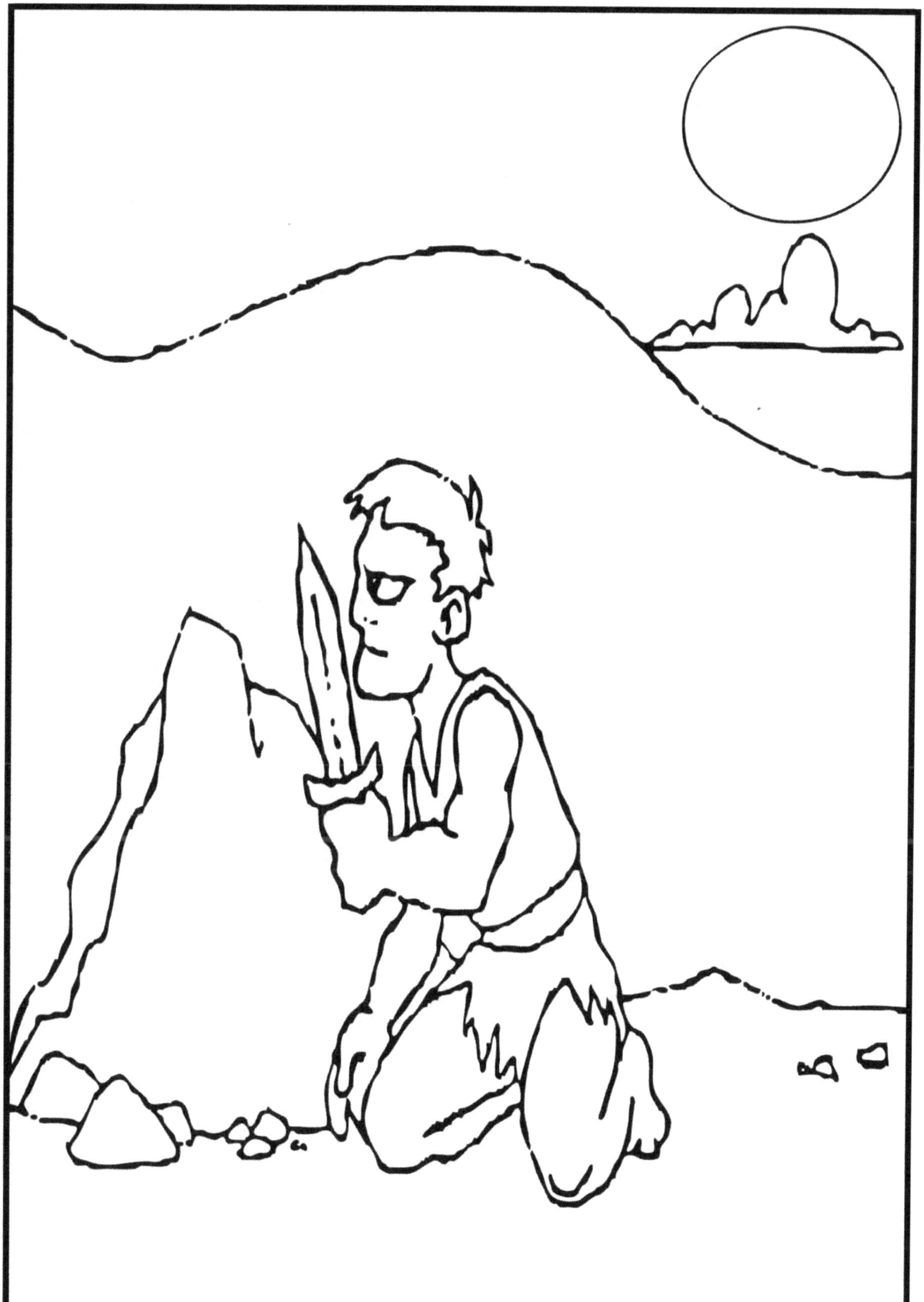

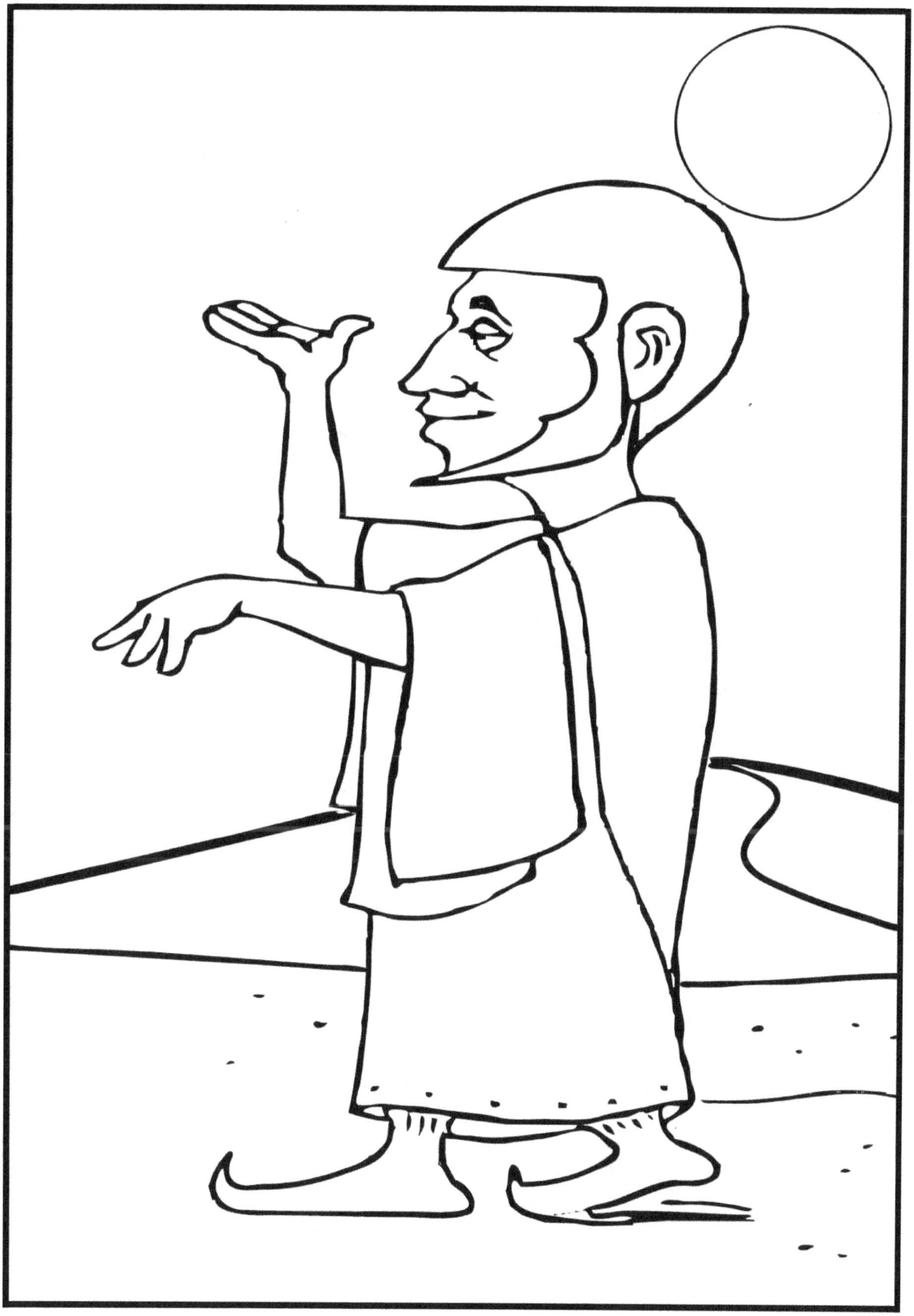

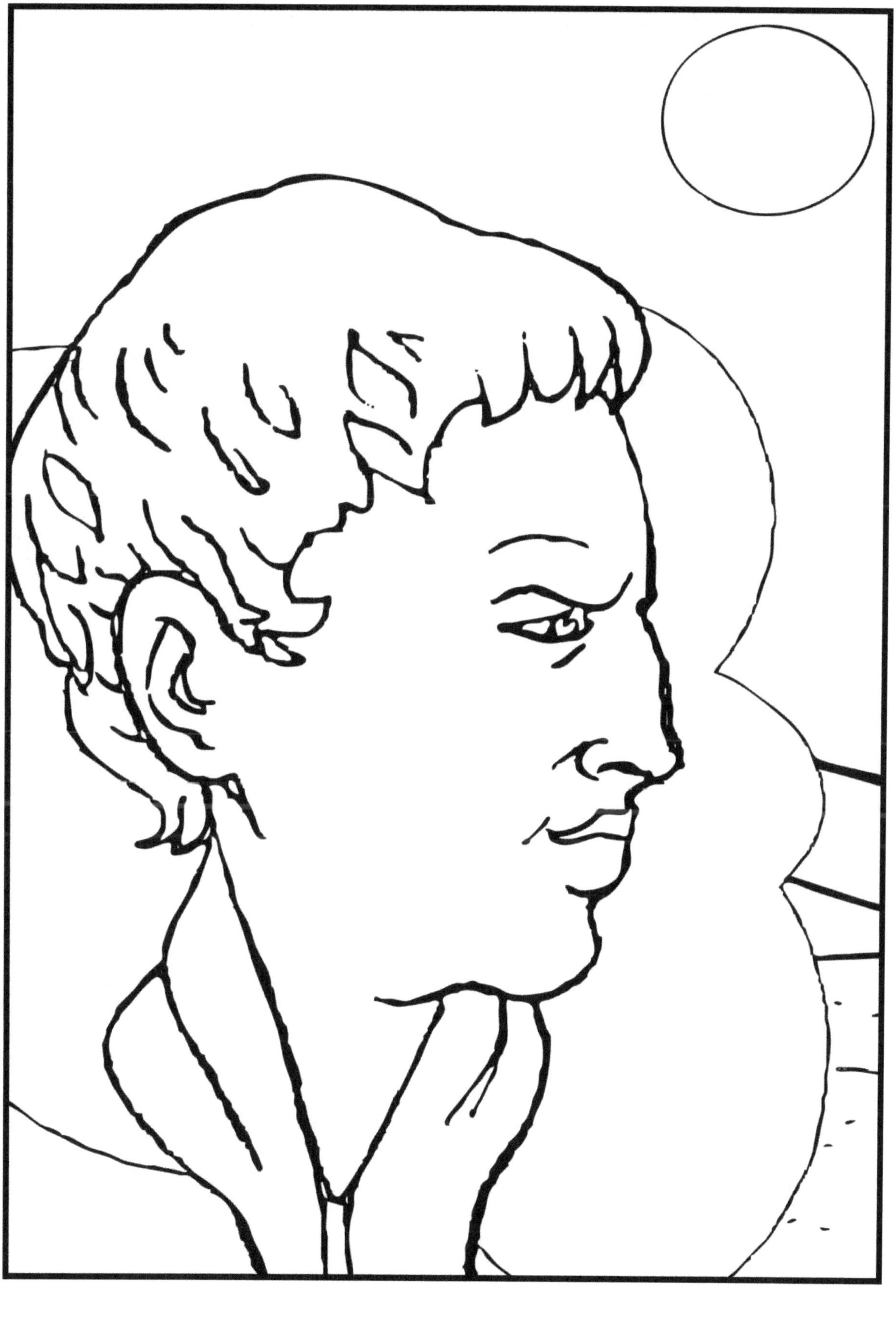

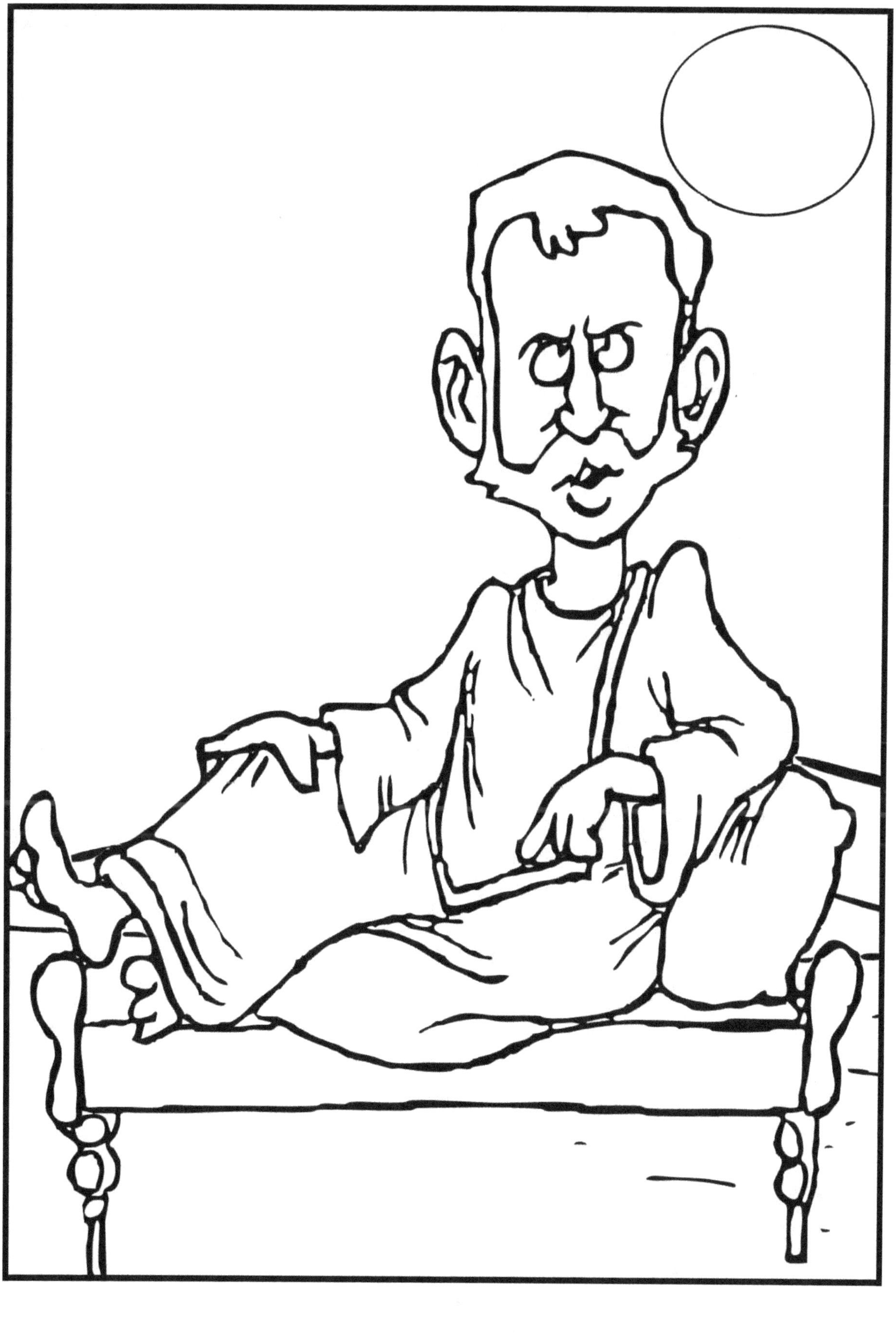

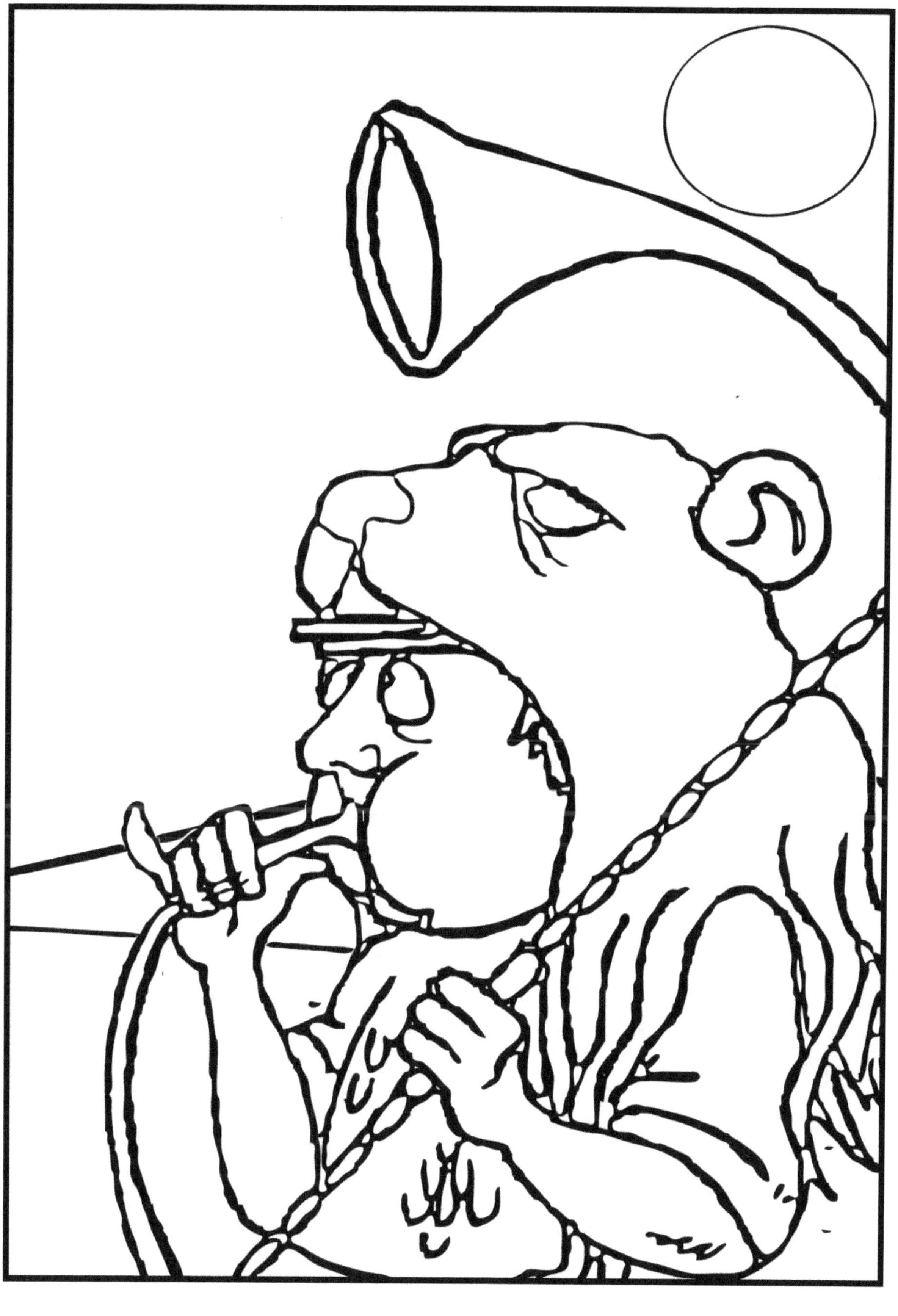

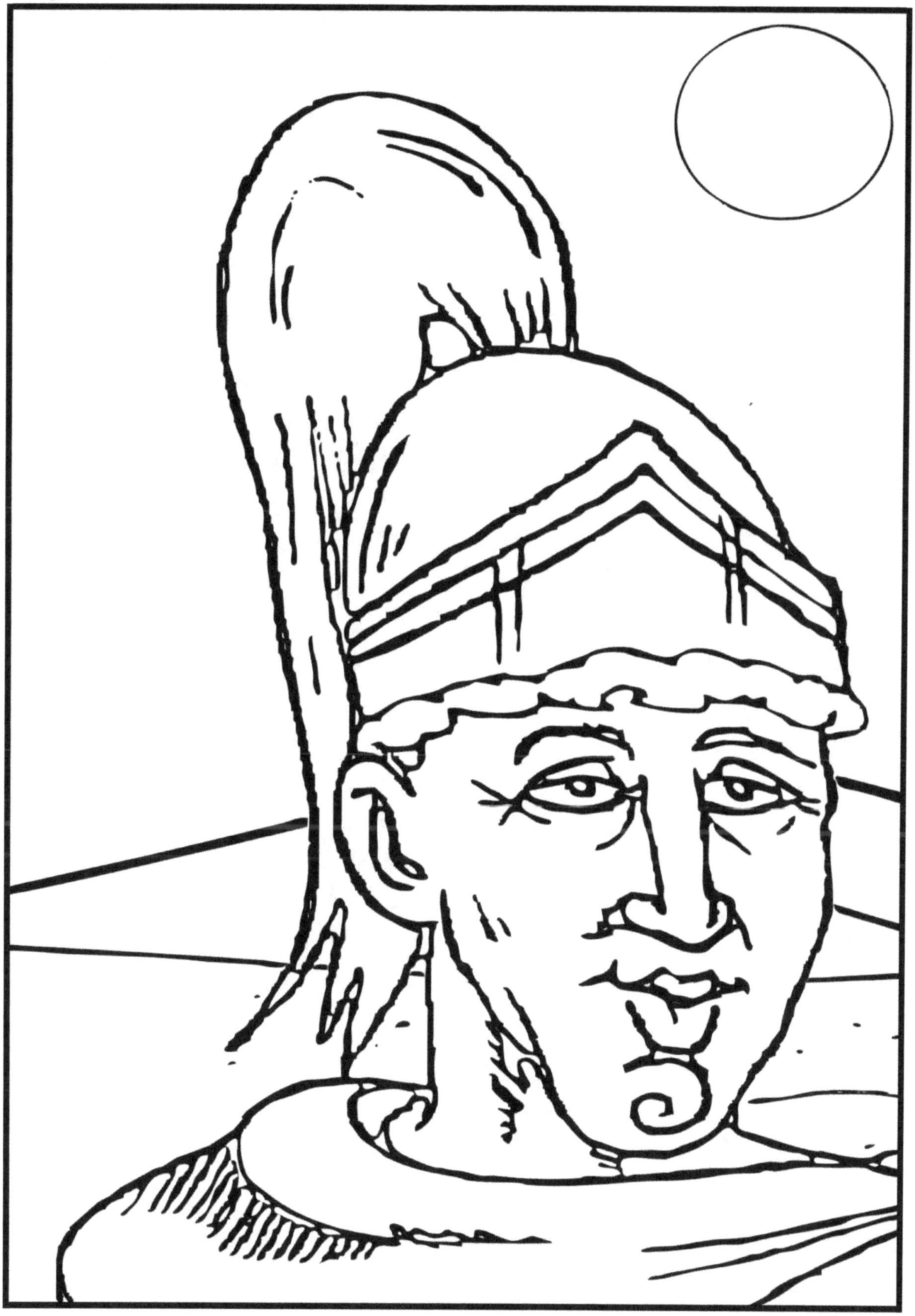

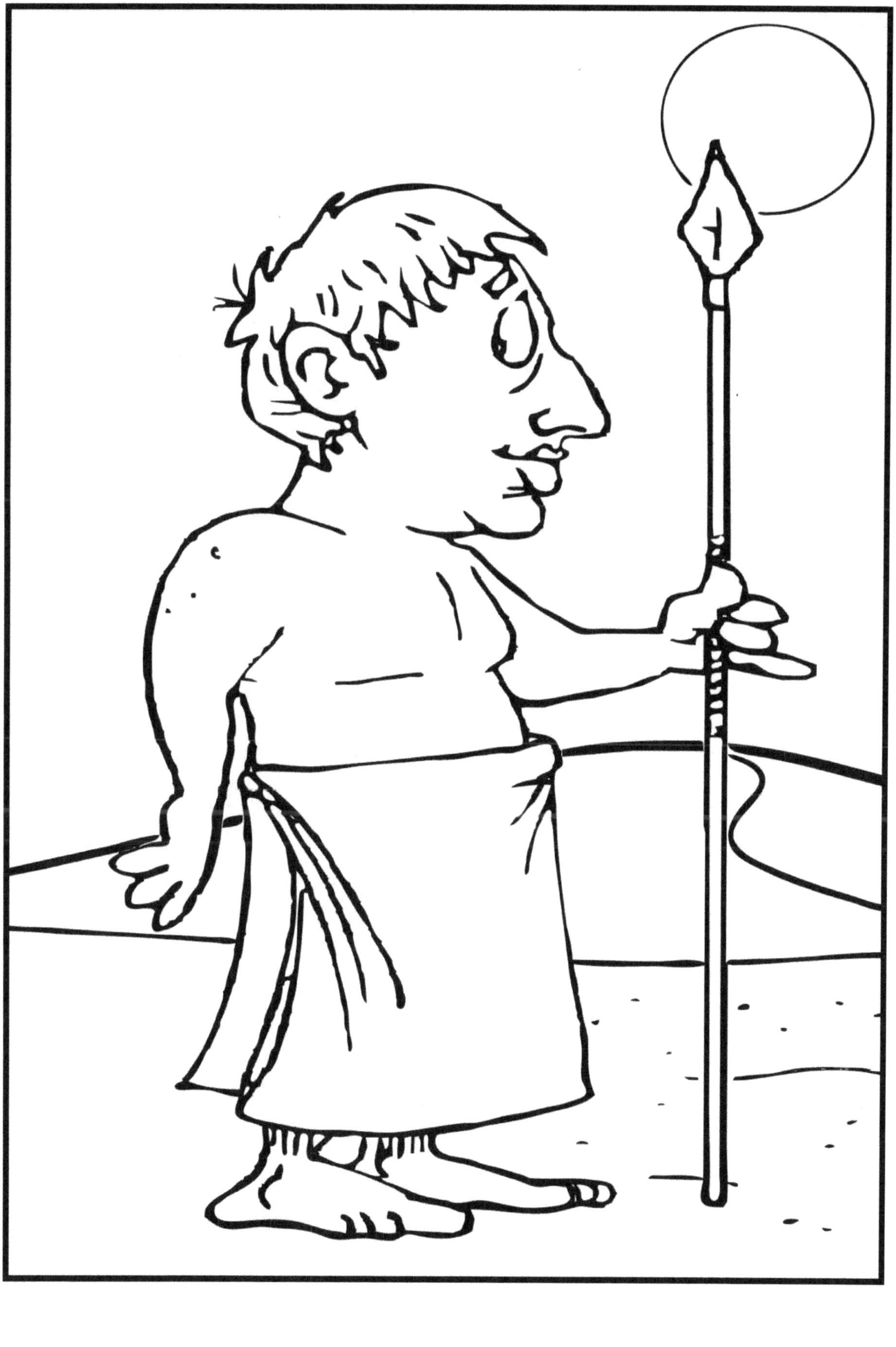

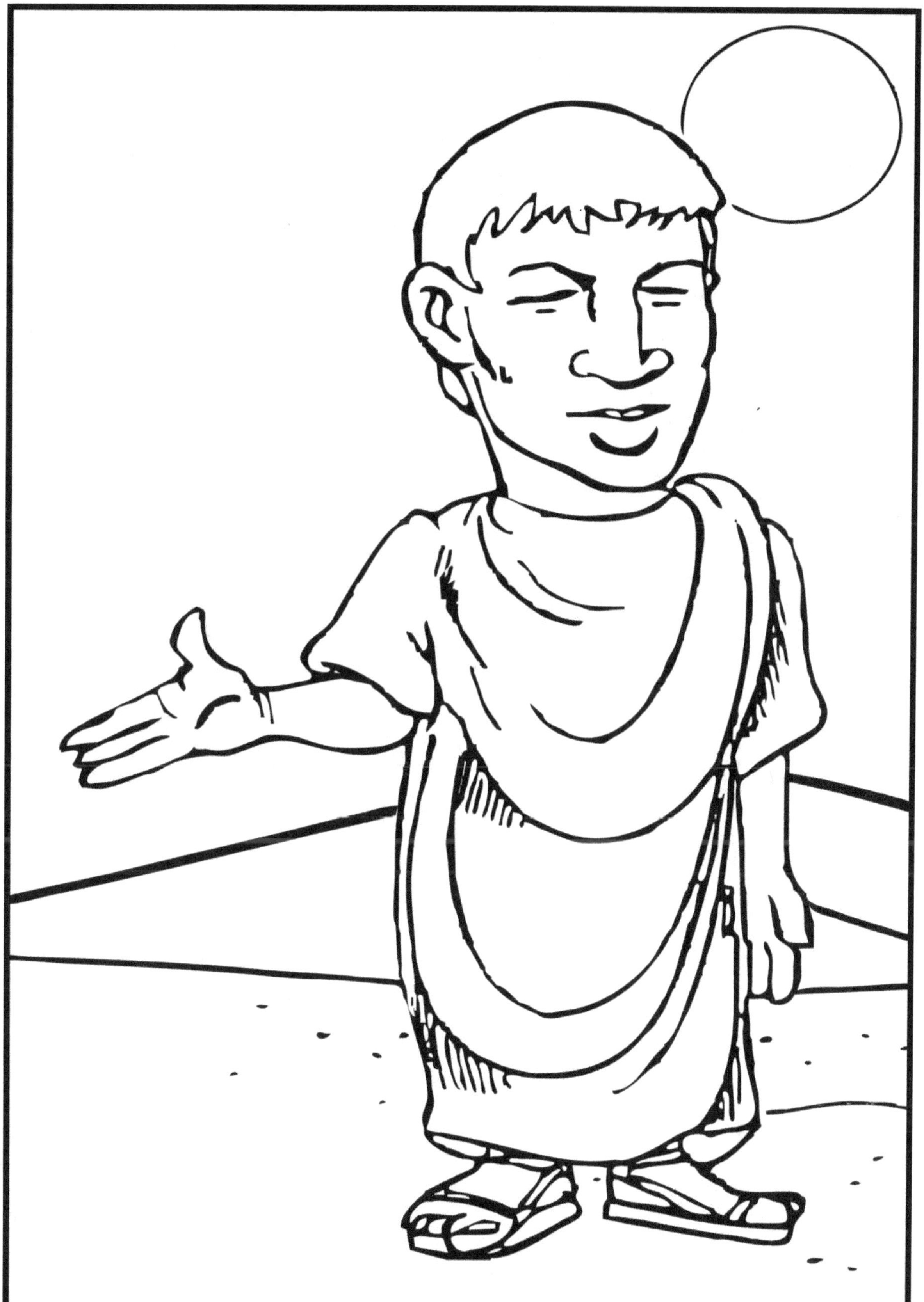

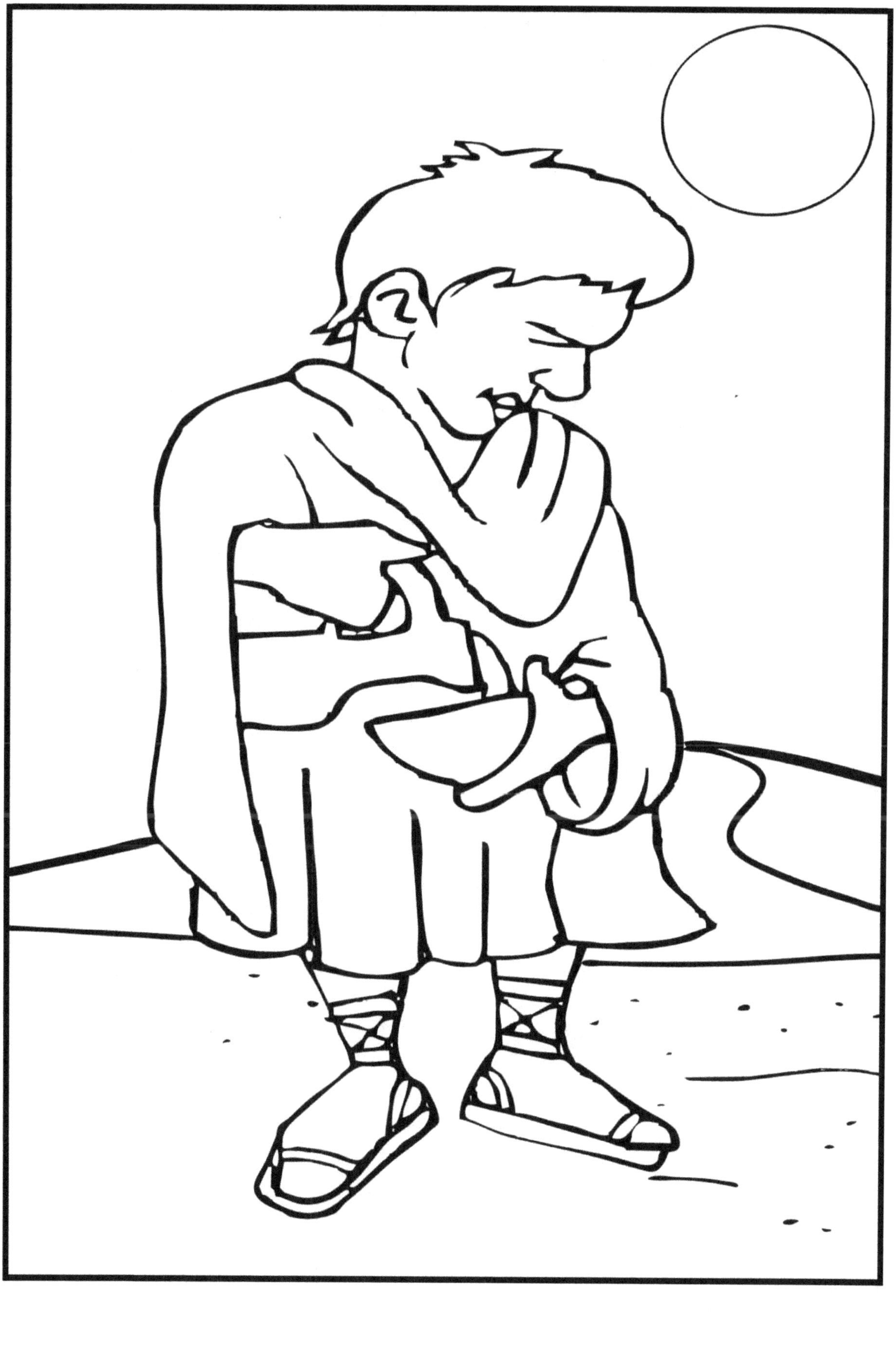

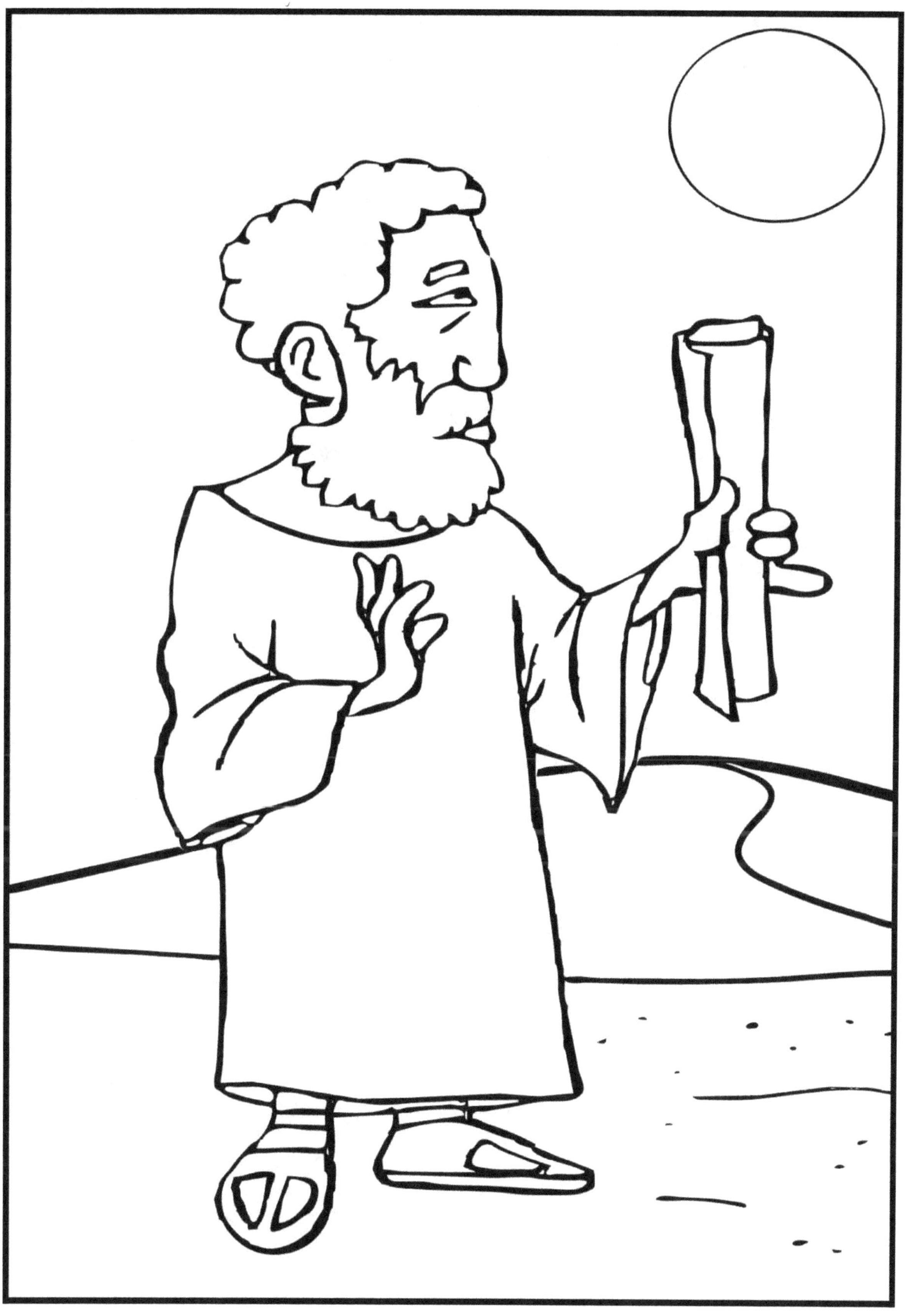

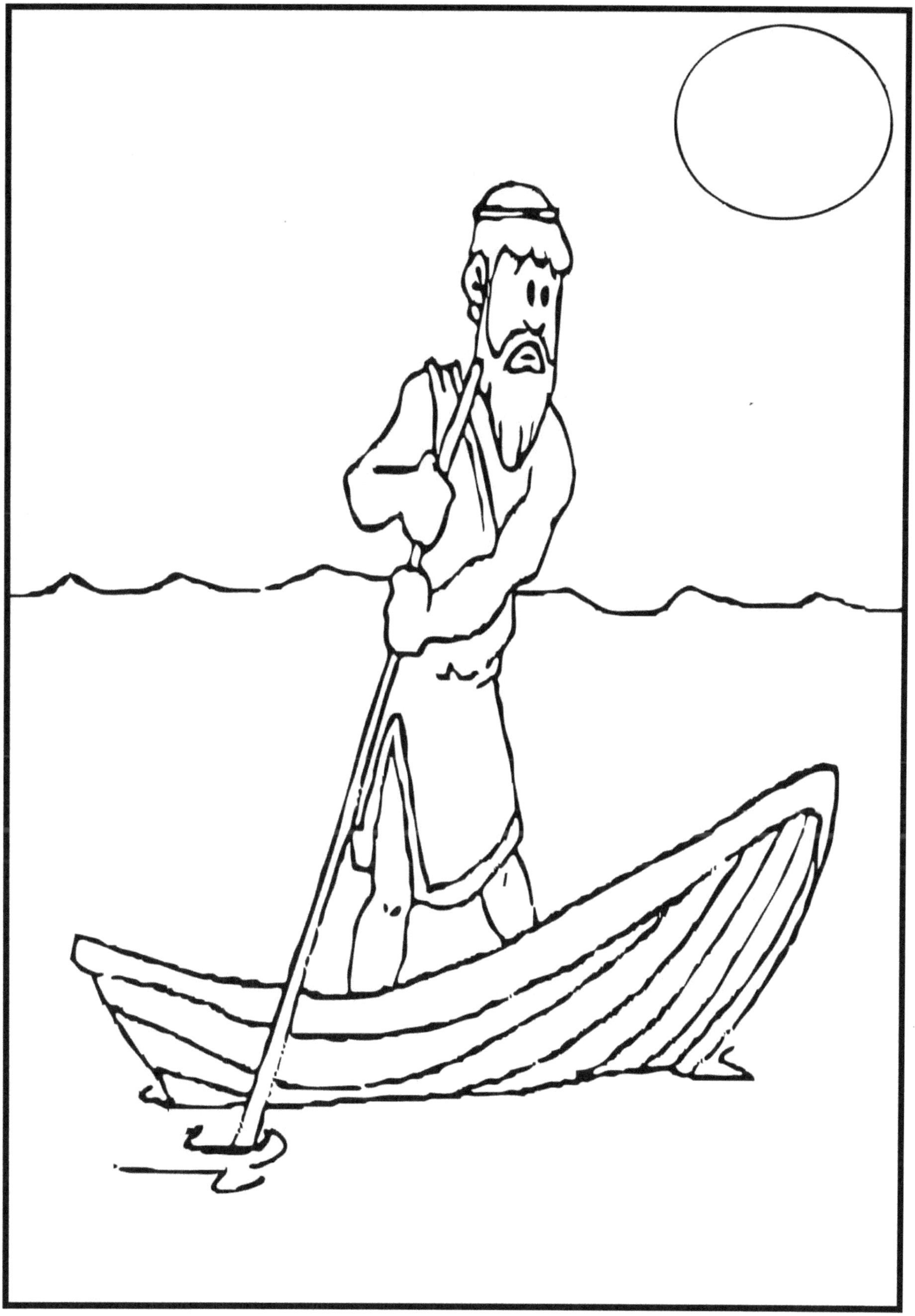

Historical Mannequin COSTUMES Coloring Book

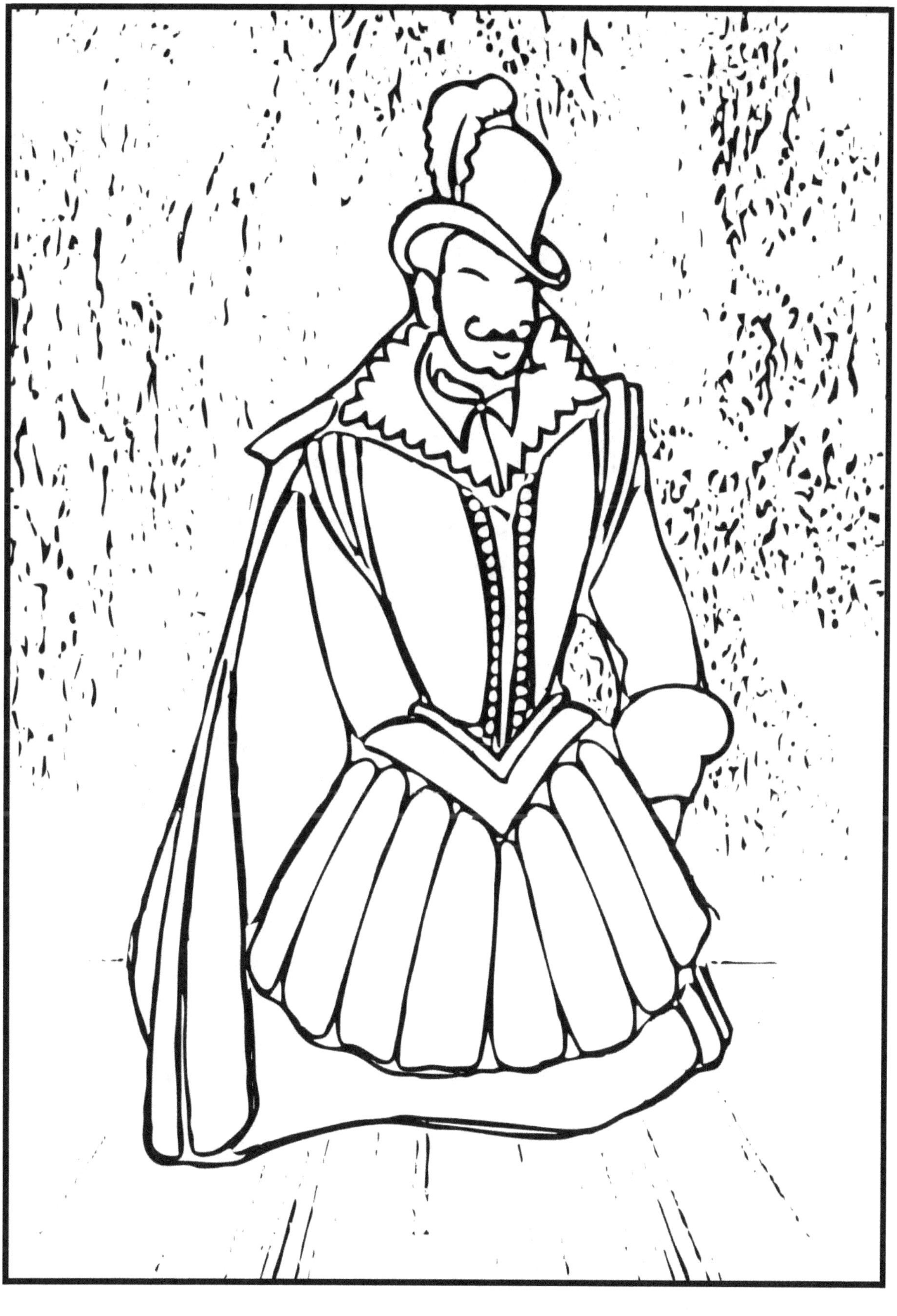

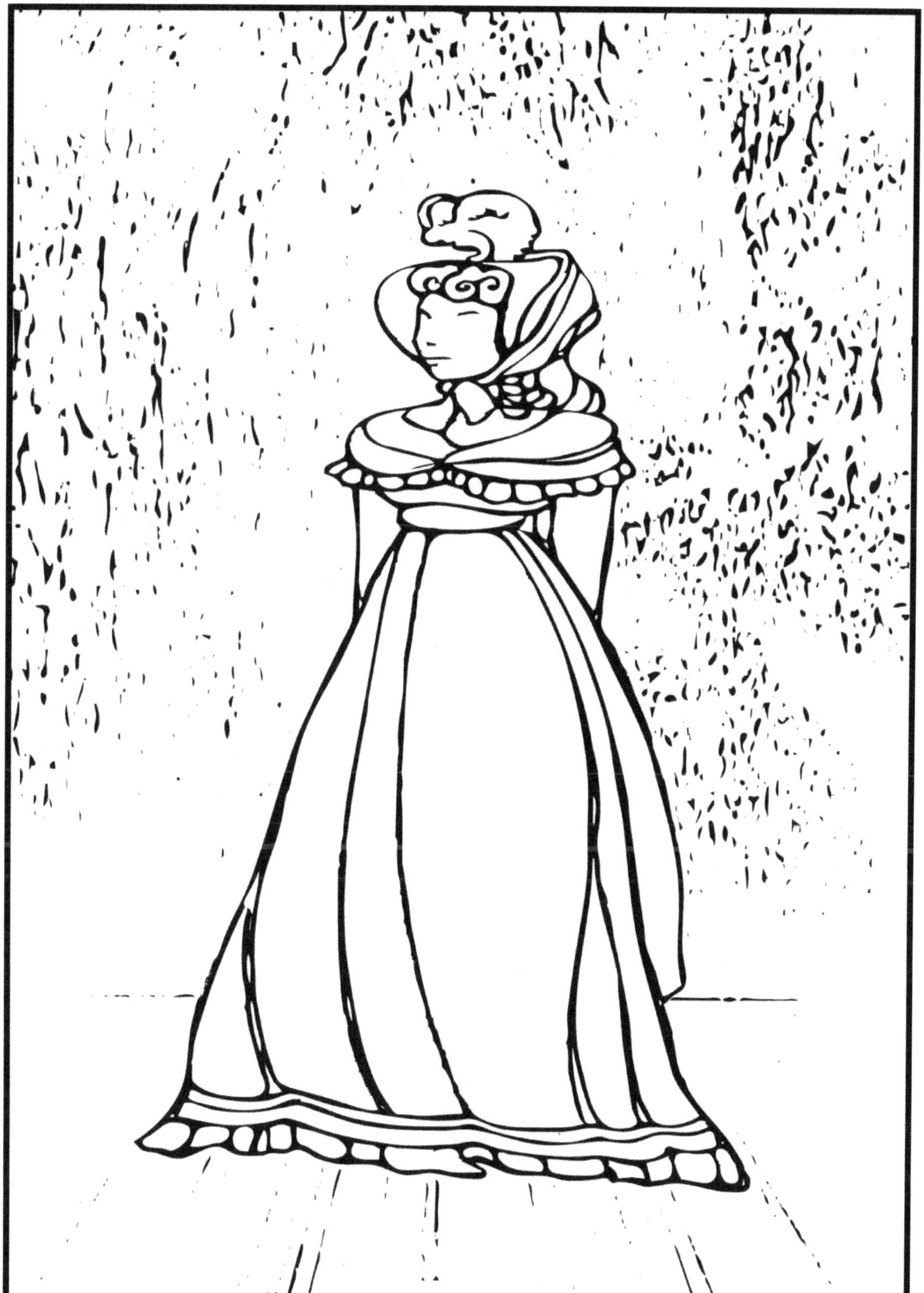

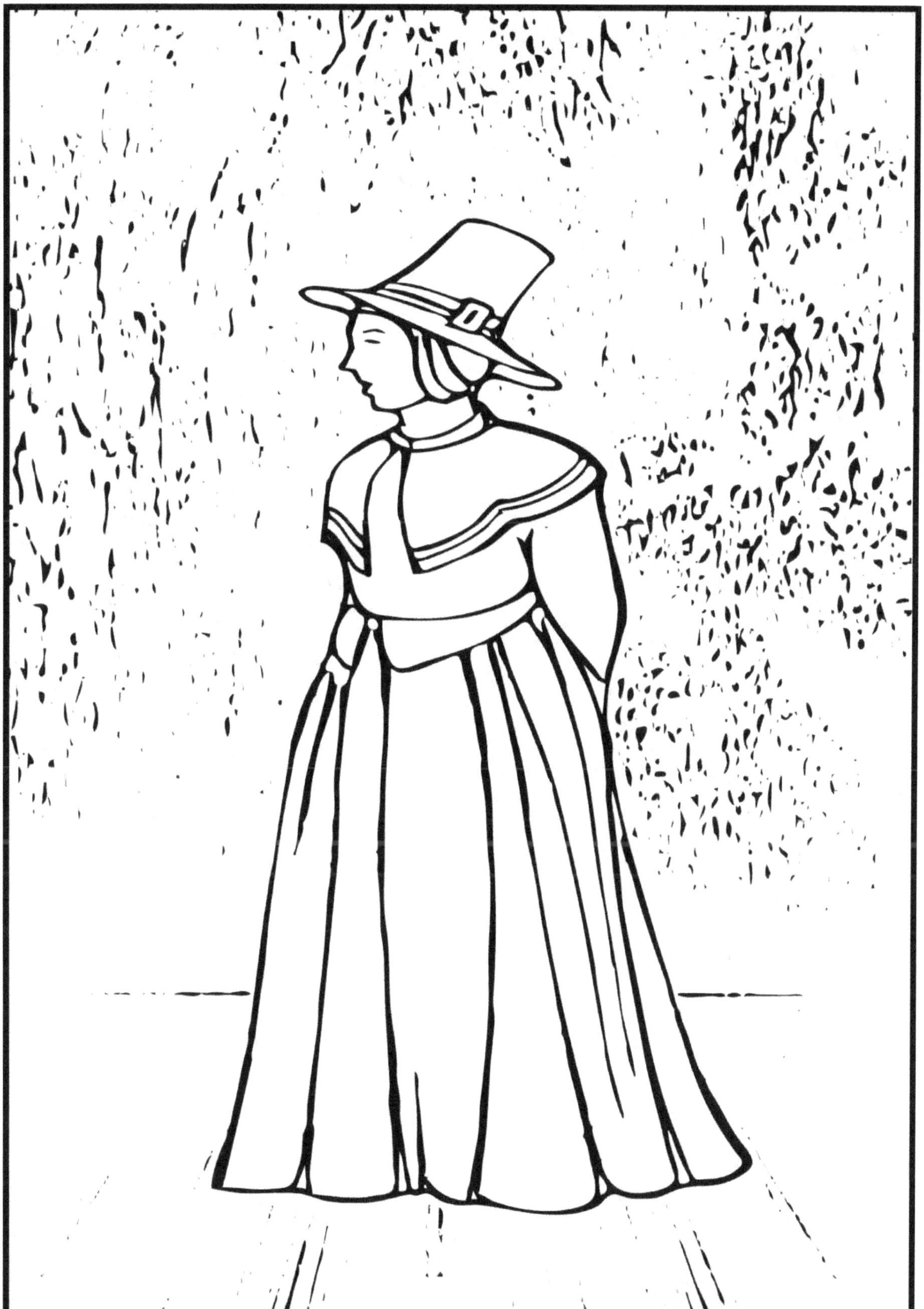

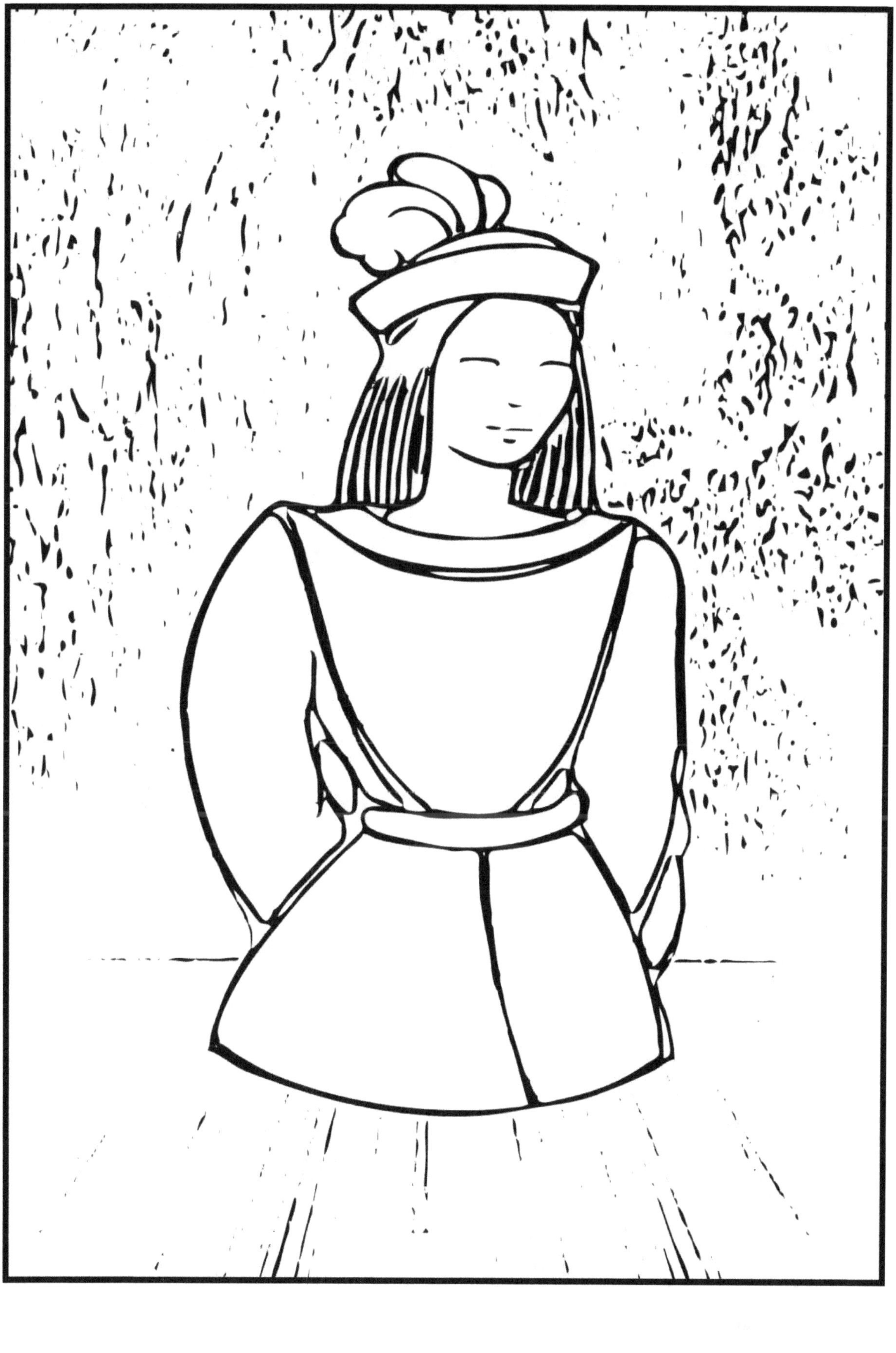

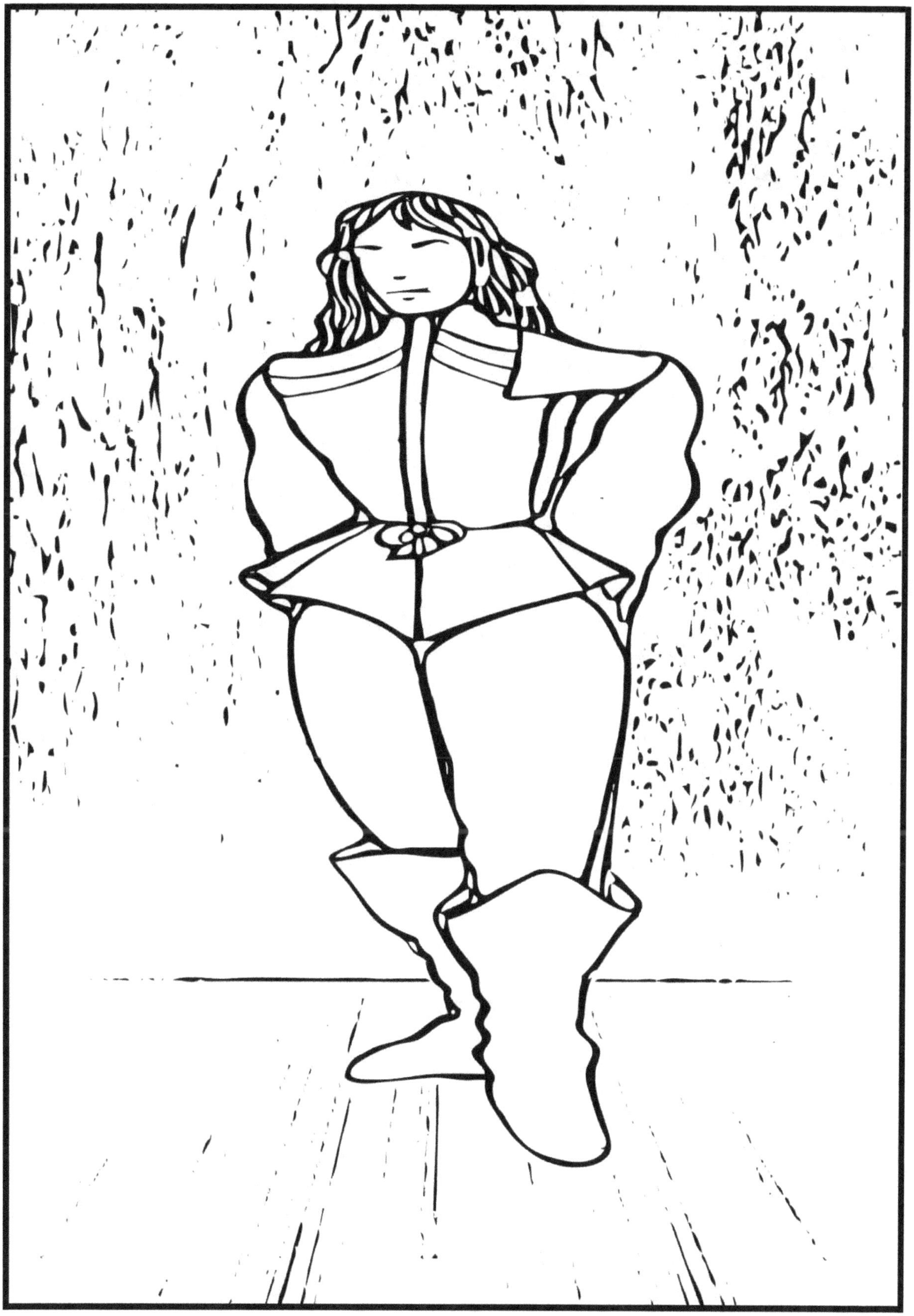

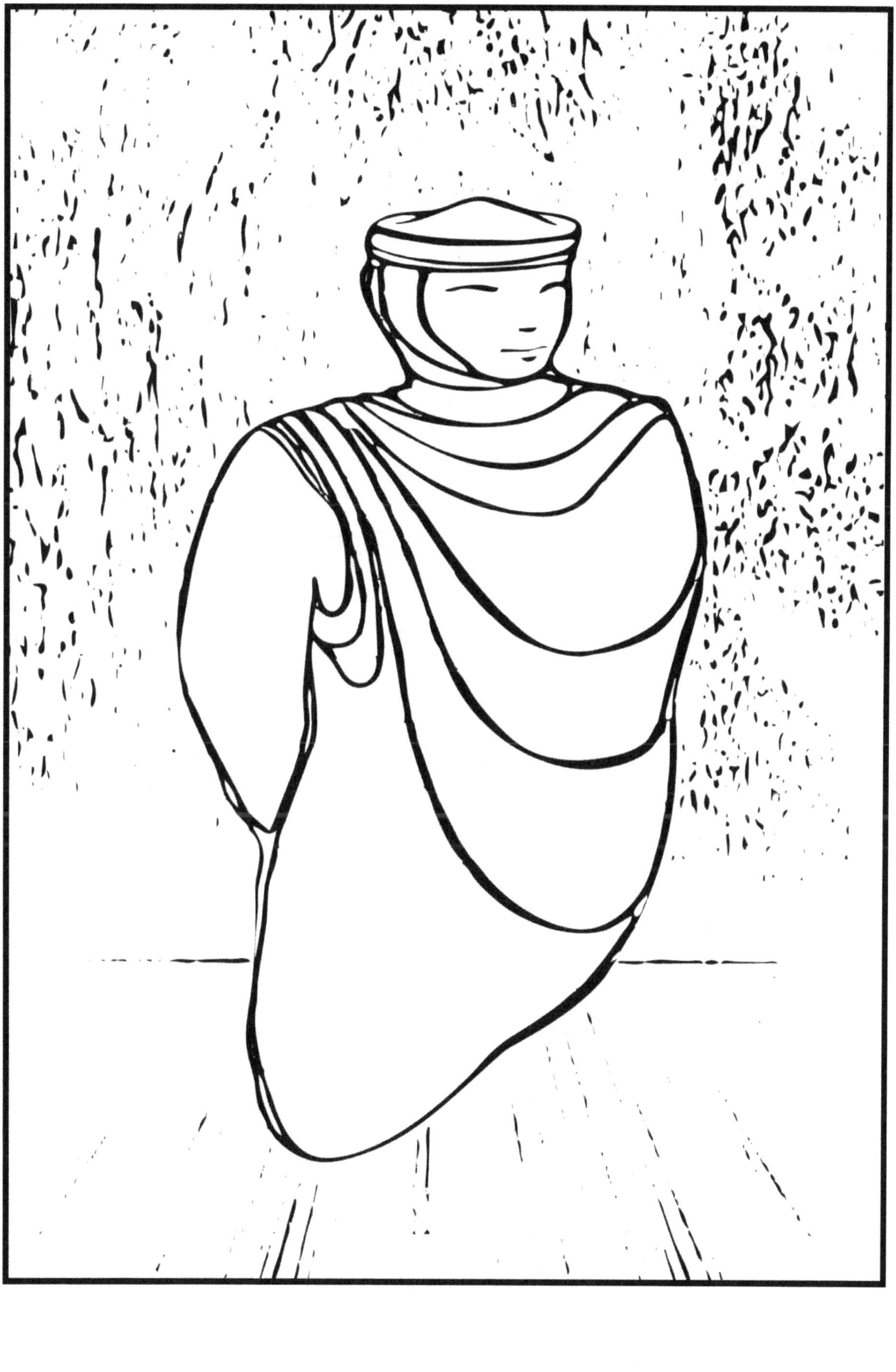

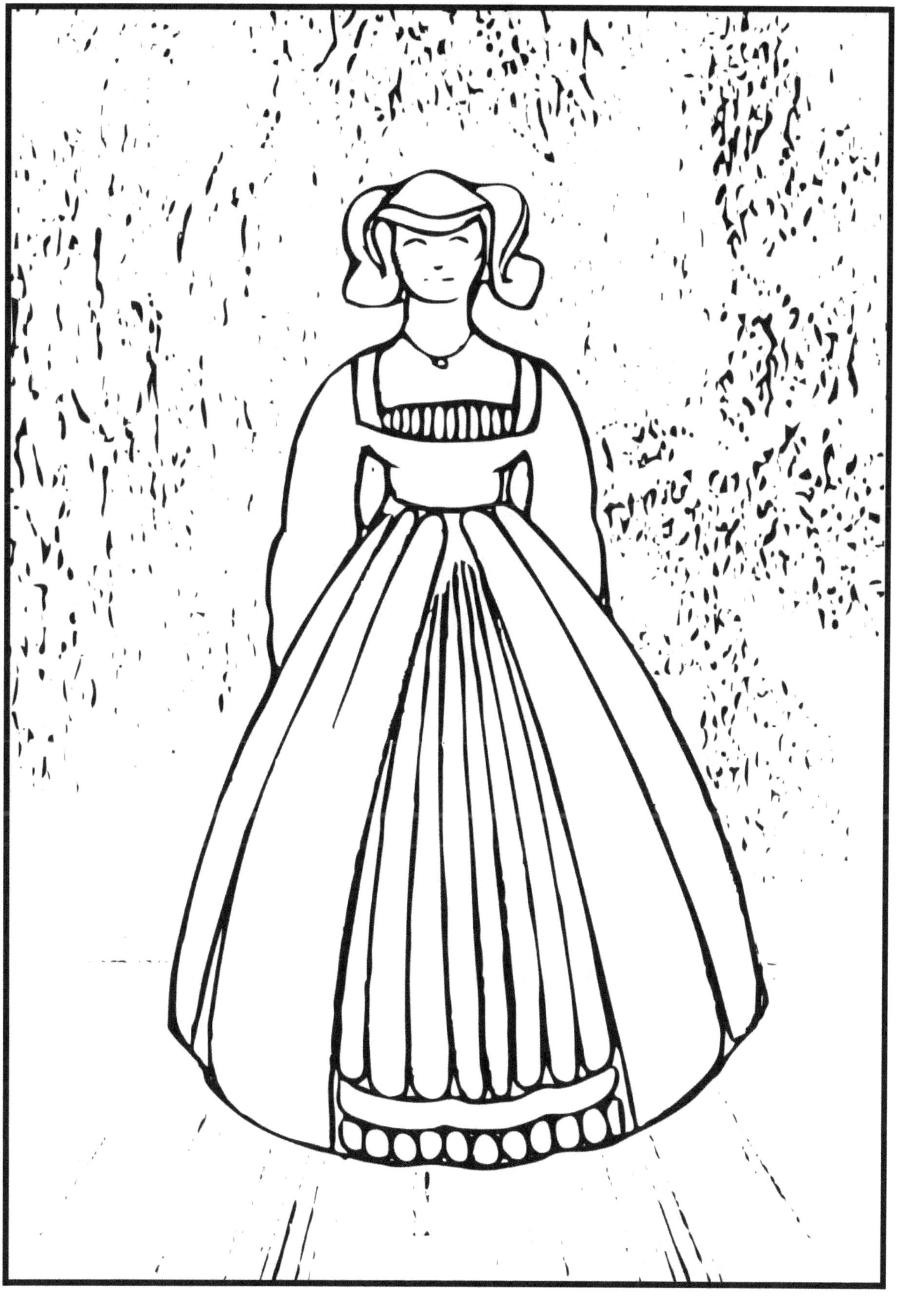

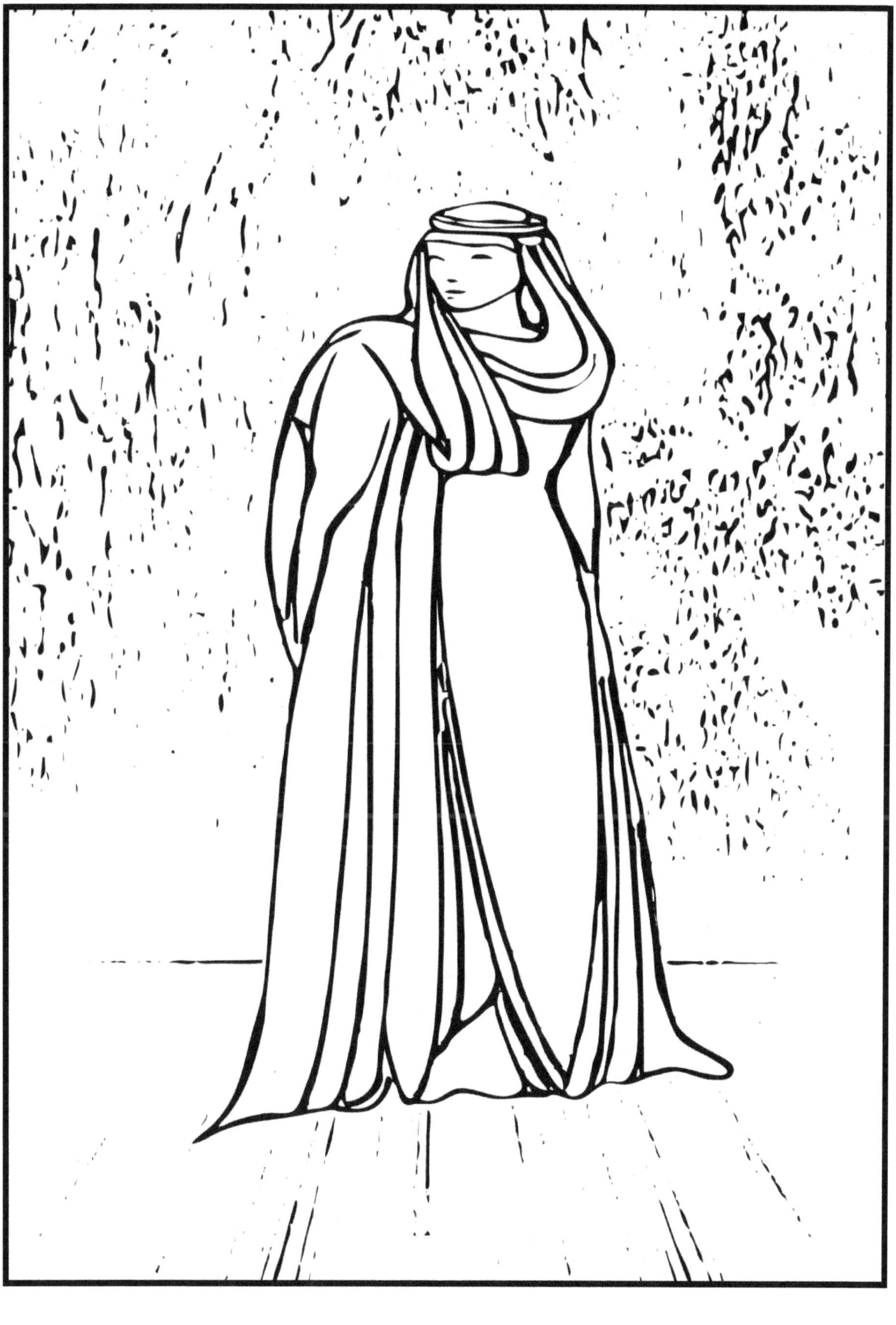

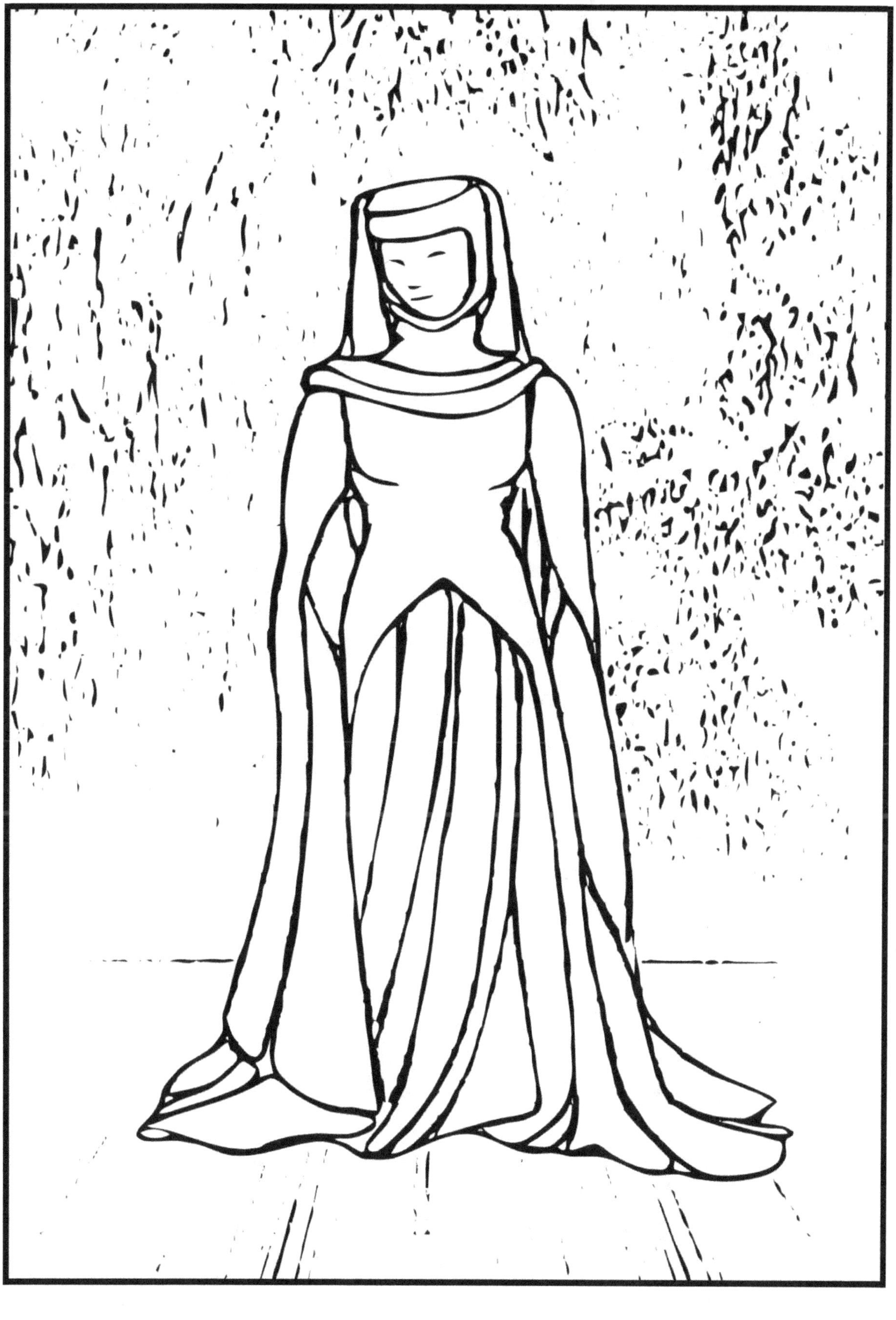

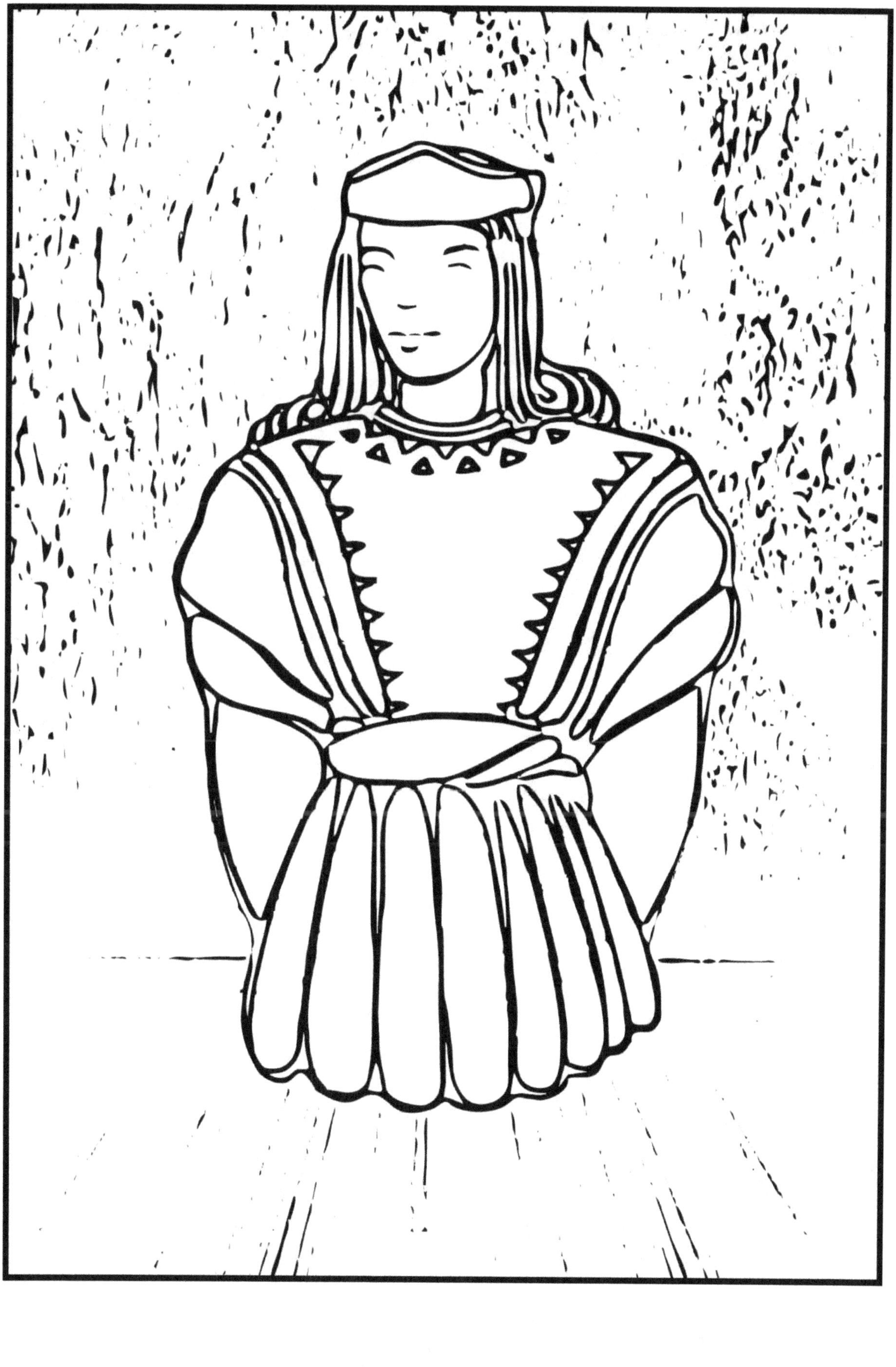

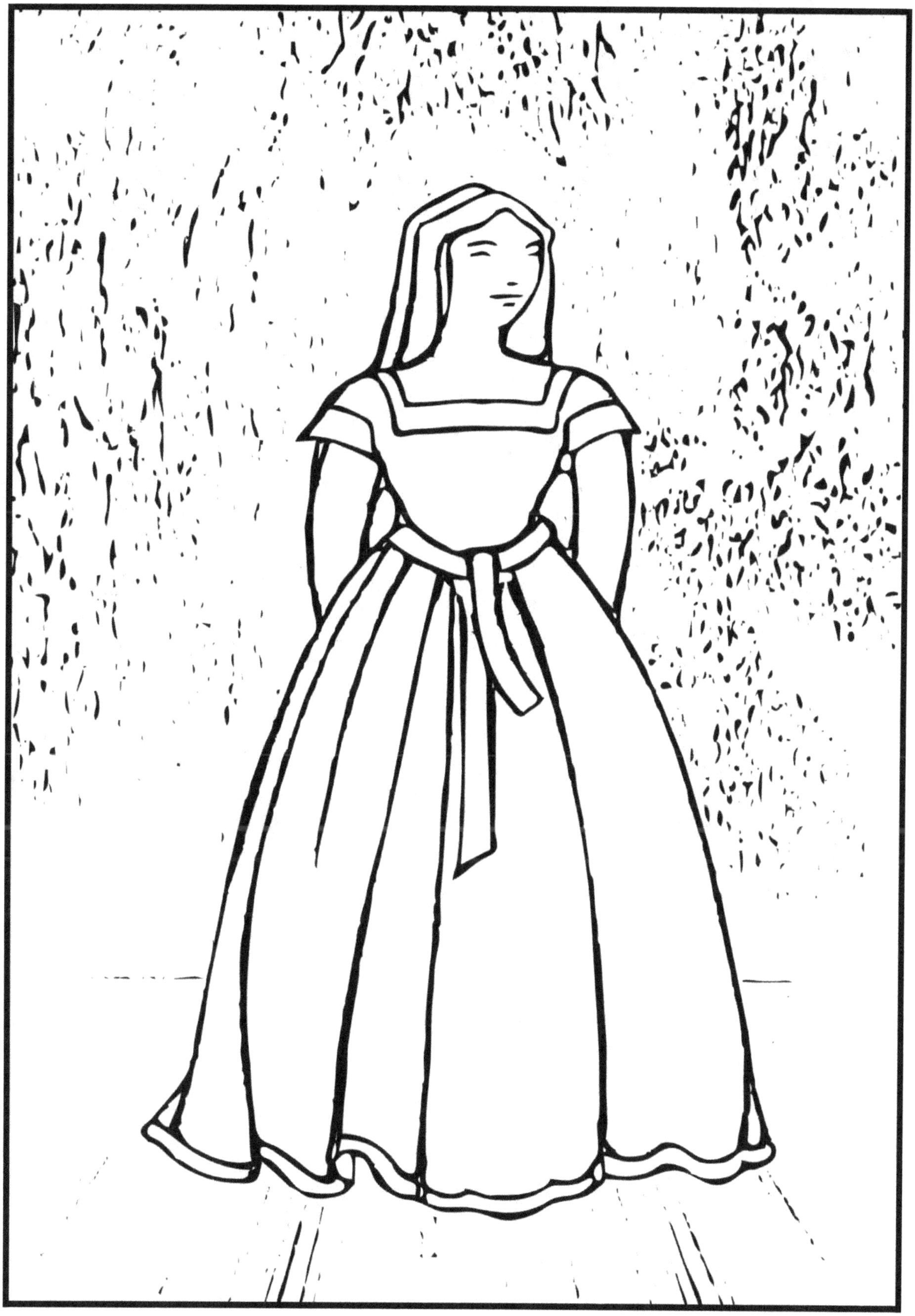

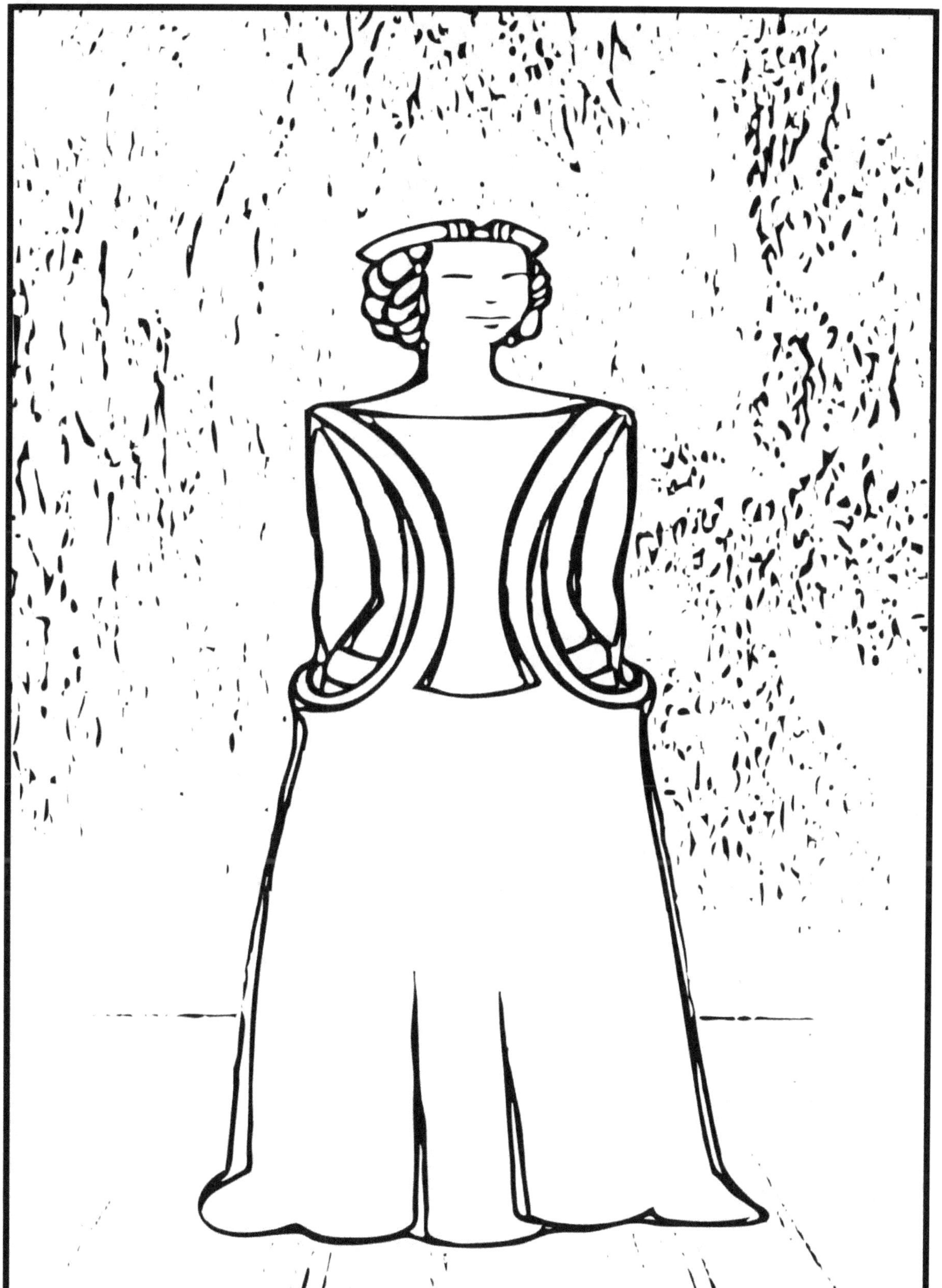

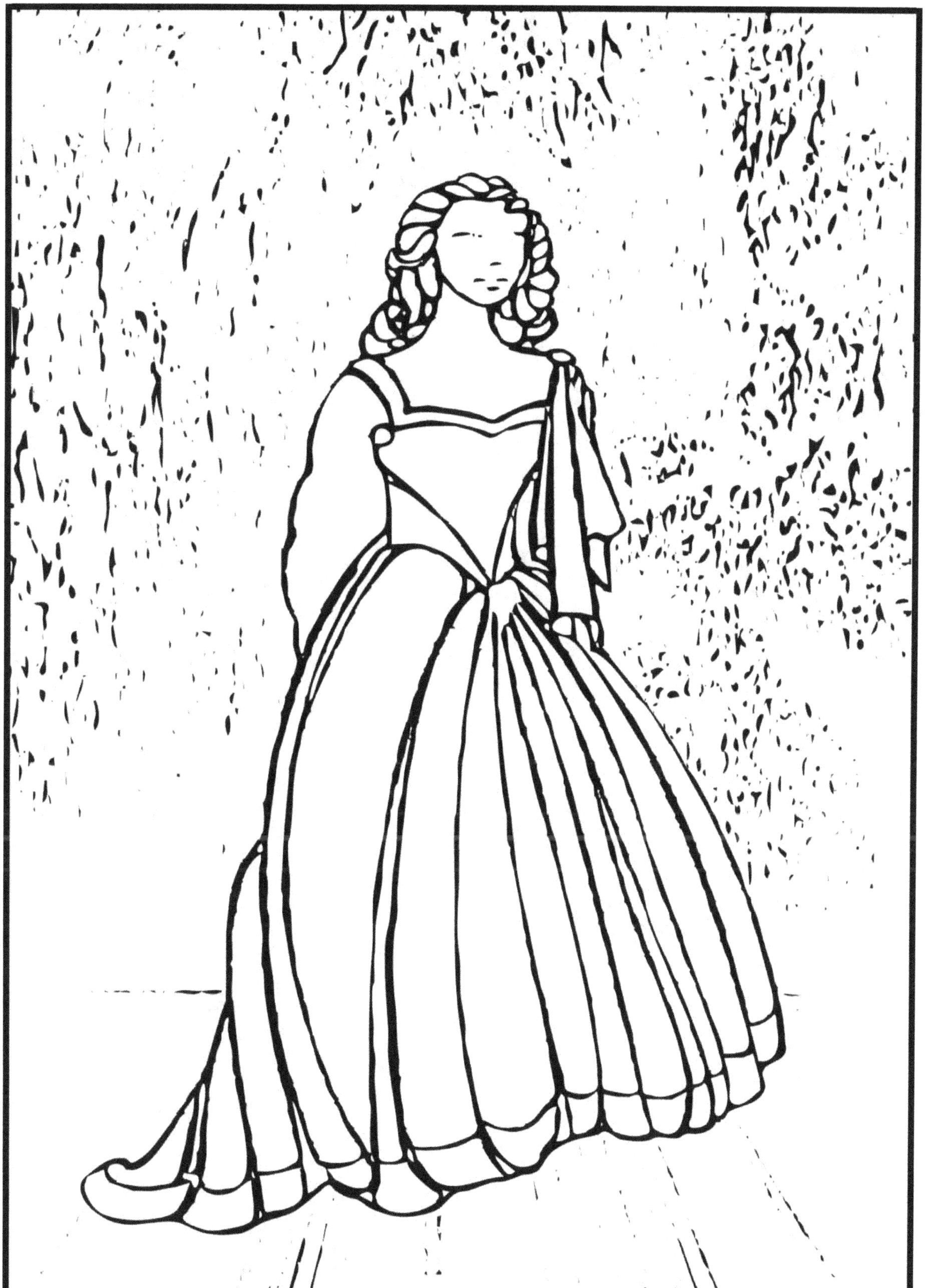

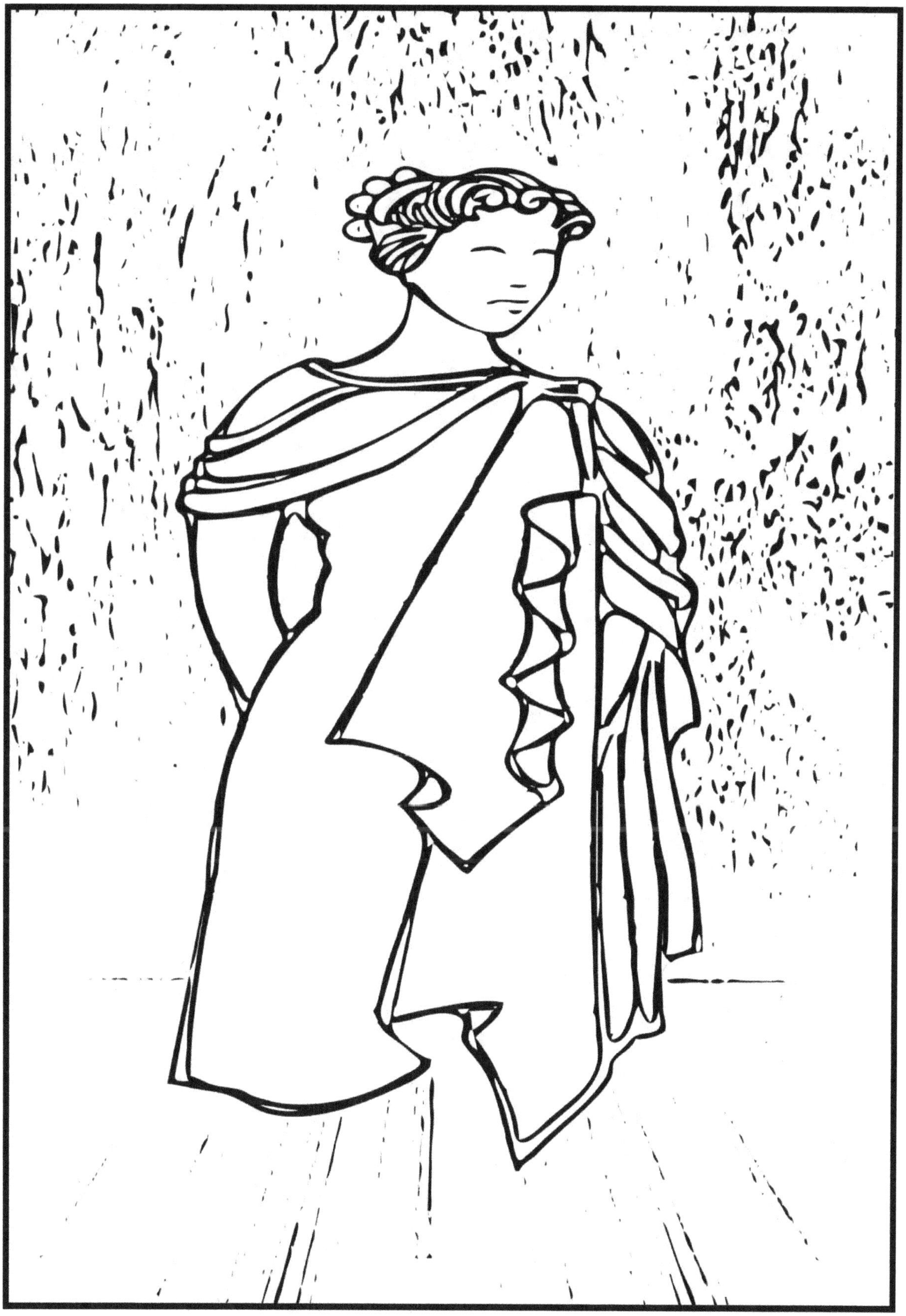

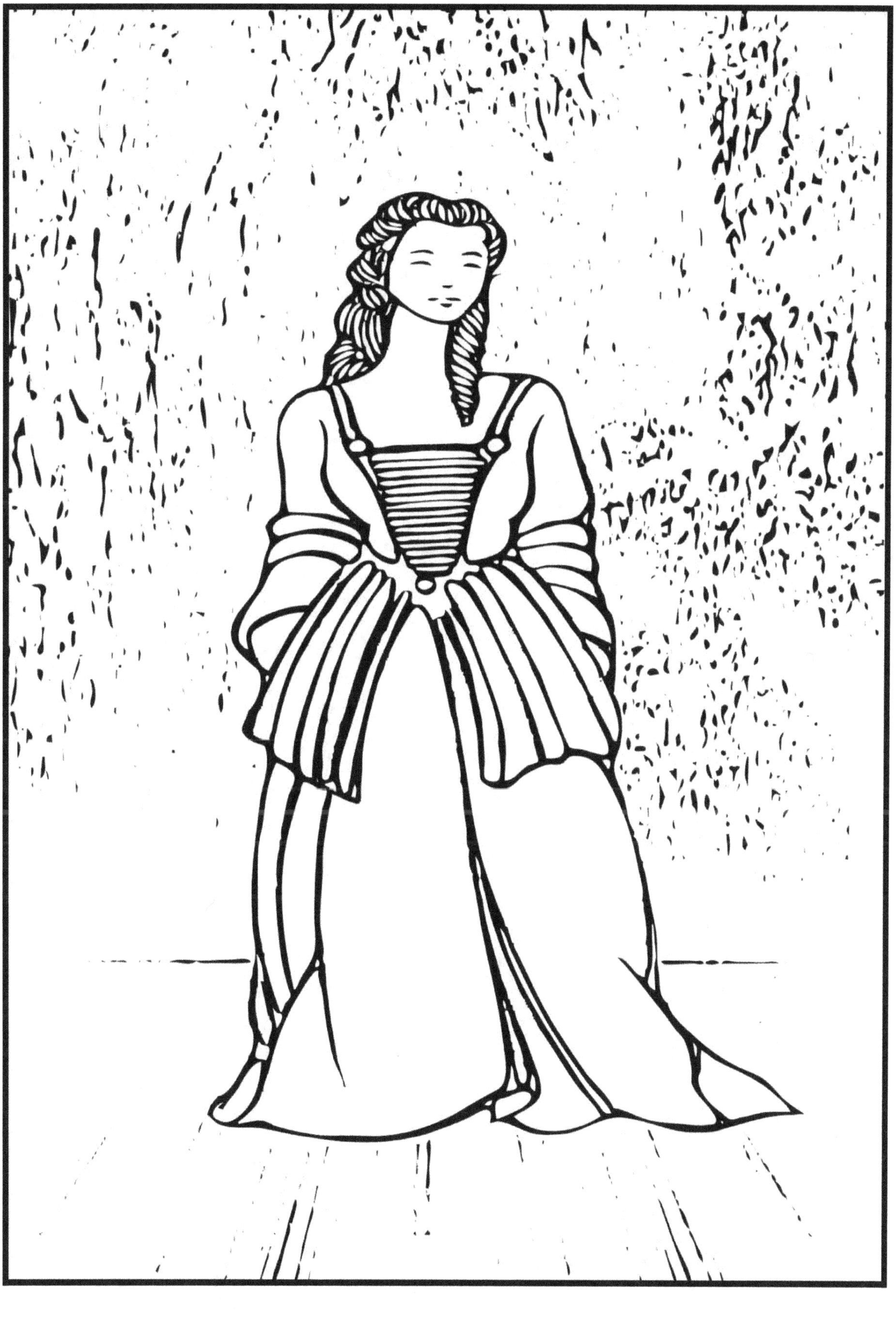

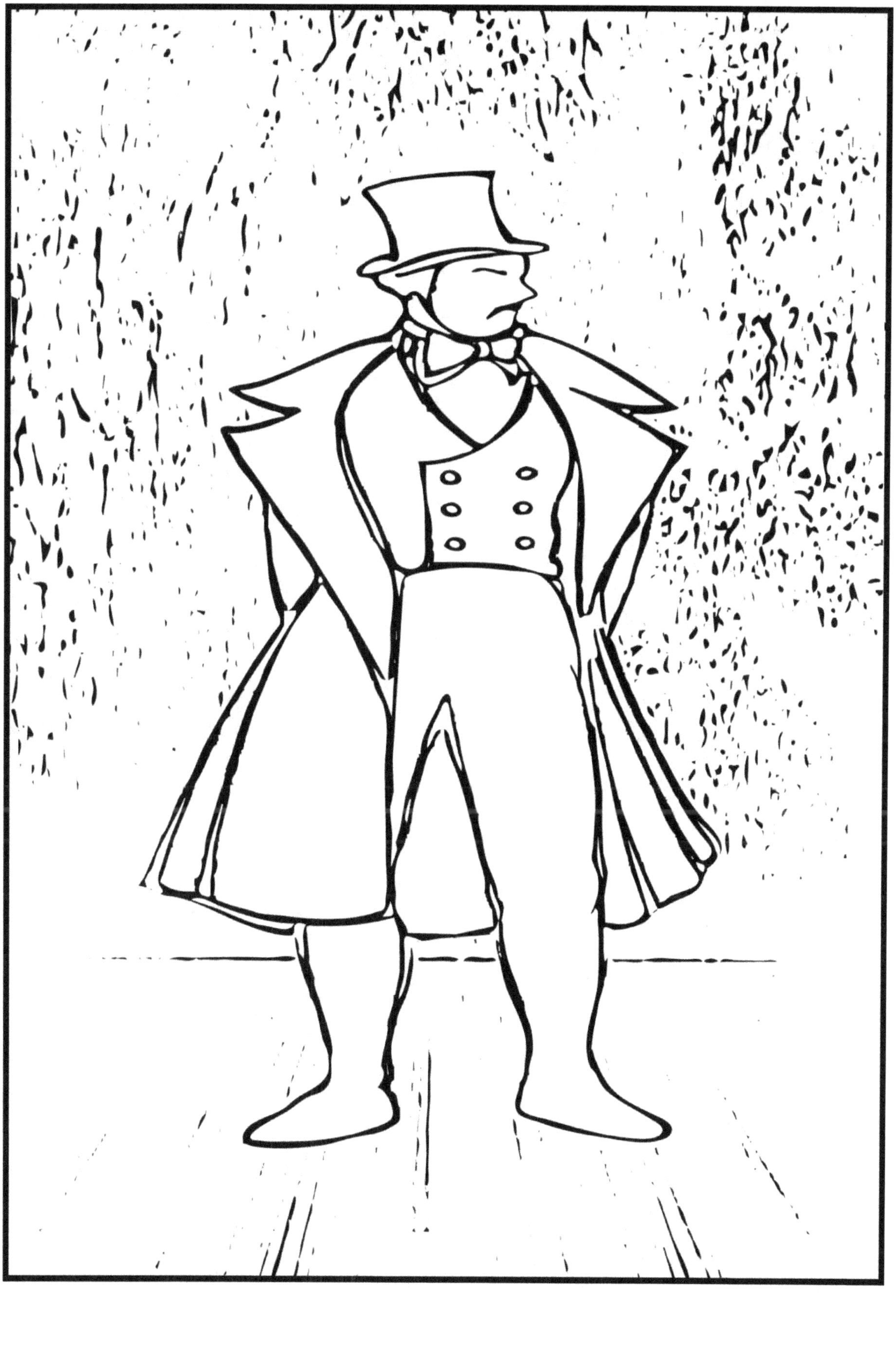

www.ingramcontent.com/pod-product-compliance
Lightning Source LLC
Chambersburg PA
CBHW081210180526
45170CB00006B/2287
9781522969792